Cecily Griffiths

ISBN 978-0-9551826-2-4

Published by

Access Books

COLCHESTER

British Library Cataloguing-in-Publication Data
A CIP catalogue record is available for this book from the British Library

Copyright © 2014 Access Books / CALA

Access Books is the publishing arm of CALA,
Colchester Adult Learning Assistance,
an educational charity, number 1095713

Typeset by Access Books. Printed and bound by Juniper House of Print, Lawford, Essex

access.books@btinternet.com

www.greyfriarscolchester.org.uk

Aerial view of the current core buildings from the north in the 1990s

Grey Friars

COLCHESTER'S FORGOTTEN CORNER
The seven lives of a special site
Joan Gurney & Alan Skinner

•

Contents

Part One – History and Development
A Quiet Corner of Colchester

Part Two - Architecture
The Georgian Family Home

Foreword

Colchester is well known for being Britain's oldest recorded town. Its Roman origins and links with Boudicca, together with the Norman castle and recently-discovered Roman Circus (unique in this country) make it an important tourist venue. The Iron Age settlement nearby (Camulodunum, home of Cunobelin, king of the Trinovantes) adds further to its heritage.

The current town stems from the construction and development of, first, the legionary fortress, followed by Colonia Victricensis (City of Victory, a town largely for military veterans and the first capital city of Roman Britain) and, after Boudicca's attack, the fully-enclosed walled town. A thousand years later the Normans built their biggest keep in Europe, including the foundations of the Roman Temple of Claudius within their own.

Turner, in his unmistakably 'misty' style, painted Colchester Castle in 1825/6 in its prominent position above the Colne river. Some church spires and towers are included and recognisable today. Few other buildings appear, but the sharp fall of the land away from the castle, and the ridge upon which the Roman wall is constructed, indicates what an almost impenetrable early fortress this must have been, perched on the top of a hill.

JMW Turner Colchester circa 1826 © The Samuel Courtauld Trust, The Courtauld Gallery London

4

However, next to the castle, enclosed within the north-eastern portion of Colchester's encircling Roman/Medieval wall, lies a relatively unrecorded and historically neglected area whose story has never been fully told.

At the heart of this quadrant in an imposing position on the crest of East Hill stands Grey Friars. It is not only a beautiful C18th neo-classical building (listed grade II*), but was for a hundred years a much-loved icon of educational excellence – and, centuries before 1755 when the house was built, seats of learning were present. Within its seven distinct lives, occupants have included friars, nuns, householders, clergy, physicians, horticulturists and students (both young and adult) as well as an industrialist.

From 2008, the building stood empty having been sold by Essex County Council, stating that they judged it to be no longer fit for the purpose of education. It is now enjoying a renaissance as a hotel, and once more its beautiful and extraordinary internal features can be enjoyed by many. Situated within easy walking distance of many interesting surviving features from across the centuries, it makes a pleasant starting point for a walking tour of the town.

The idea for this book sprang from an exhibition and series of guided tours of Grey Friars which the authors conducted in September 2007 as part of the national Heritage Open Days 'Free to Explore' annual event.

This was during the building's sad last months as the headquarters of Colchester's award-winning Adult Community College. A large number of people attended, not only past students and staff of the college and local residents, but also alumnae of Colchester County High School for Girls whose Preparatory and Junior Departments had occupied the building from 1920 to 1957.

It was a remarkable weekend; many visitors were emotionally affected by memories and reminders of its history and architecture, which we were strongly requested to record. So here begins the story.

J.D.Gurney
A.V.Skinner
Colchester 2014

Geographical location
of the Grey Friars site

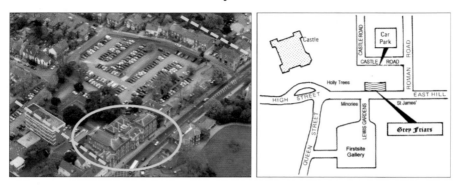

The Grey Friars building, as it now stands, is situated at the eastern end of High Street (in the section formerly called Frere Street), at the crest of East Hill, post code CO1 1UG.

The core of the complex (circled above) is the magnificent house of 1755 and 1780, a fascinating example of Georgian architecture, with its later extensions.

The area explored by this book (part of which is shown within the dotted lines) is larger than the present site. It extends from the High Street northwards to the town wall, beyond Castle Road and Roman Road.

It covers the original Grey Friars grounds, believed to have been bounded by the north-east corner of the Roman wall, the Castle Park side of Castle Road and the section of road where High Street becomes East Hill.

The contents of this book set out what the authors have so far discovered about the origin, development, use and occupation of this part of town, but there is much more. The website www.greyfriarscolchester.org continues the learning journey, to which all interested parties are invited courtesy of the education charity CALA (Colchester Adult Learning Assistance).

This book is part of a 'Sharing History' project including an interactive website and allied educational activities. The CALA charity gratefully acknowledges financial support from the Heritage Lottery Fund.

Colchester 1990s, looking west along High Street from top of East Hill and part of Grey Friars site (shown within yellow lines).
© CALA/Access Books

Part One

•

History and Development

•

A Quiet Corner of Colchester

Aerial view of part of Grey Friars site seen from the south in the 1990s

1
C1st to C13th • The Romans to the Friars

Before the Romans, the original Celtic place name for the area was Camuldunon, meaning 'The Fortress of Camulos", who was the Celtic War God whose name means 'powerful'. The area belonged to the Trinovantes tribe. The Romans must have been comfortable with this as they simply Romanised the name to Camulodunum.

Modern-day Gosbeck's Farm (to the south-west, on the Maldon Road) was the site of the royal palace of Cunobelin. The Romans had allowed Cunobelin to 'rule' the south-eastern corner of Britain until the Celtic surrender to the might of Claudius's forces in AD43 when the full invasion took place. This area was later developed to include a large temple and a theatre.

The colony (or 'colonia') set up where Colchester's town centre now stands, must once have been something of a rather quiet, semi-rural scene. It had been open and relatively undefended since its establishment, developed from a military base which had been set up circa AD43 in a commanding position on the top of a rise. The Temple of Claudius was built just outside the fortress, in the north-east portion of the colonia circa AD44, adjacent to the area which was to become Grey Friars. It was basically a civilian development, forming the first capital of the province.

The inhabitants' tranquillity was shattered in AD60/61 when, as a result of Rome's insulting and barbaric treatment of her tribe and family, Boudicca (the Iceni queen) led her forces to destroy the defenceless colonia.

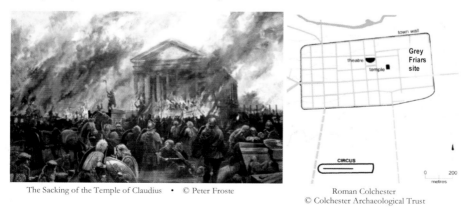

The Sacking of the Temple of Claudius • © Peter Froste

Roman Colchester
© Colchester Archaeological Trust

10

Following this devastating destruction, the inadequate previous boundaries were transformed into full military defences with banks, foundations, interval towers and monumental gateways. Thus, for the first time, the area later to become Grey Friars was enclosed within the north-east corner of the walls, between East Gate and Duncan's Gate.

Peter Froste's © conjecture of Roman Colchester, courtesy Colchester Archaeological Trust (Grey Friars site outlined)

Around AD70 saw the first phase of the rebuilding of the town, a restored temple, the first city wall in Britain, a number of important religious sites and many public facilities. Londinium (also recovering from an attack by Boudicca) eventually became the capital, but Colchester retained cult status (as 'Colonia Victricensis') until the collapse of Roman rule circa AD410.

The area later to become the Grey Friars site, shown between the arrows on the next plan, had its shape dictated partly by the position of the Roman wall to the north and east, and the main Roman street to the south. Its original western boundary has never been accurately located.

The street leading south from Duncan's Gate, however, may give an indication of a possible original boundary. If we assume that pre-existing features, such as earthworks and roads are often used as convenient markers for later boundaries, the fact that the street can be seen to divert slightly to the west gives us a clue. For in later plans and drawings of the area, this anomaly can be seen, with, variously, hedges, paths and boundaries shown with the same divergence to the west (see chapter 3 of part 1 of this book).

11

What we can be sure of, however, is that the majority of the Grey Friars site was eventually to be located within the north-east corner of the town wall, and its western boundary was somewhere between the eastern wall and the Norman castle earthworks, which were built around the site of the Temple of Claudius marked in the diagram below.

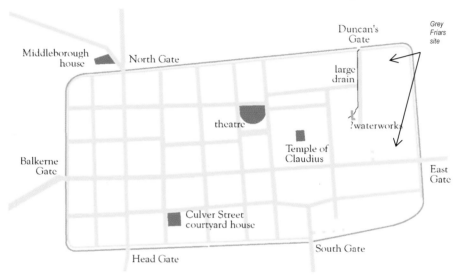

Roman Colchester, street plan taken from archaeological evidence, courtesy Colchester Archaeological Trust ©

Little is known of the site during the period between the end of the Roman occupation and the arrival of the Normans in around 1066 (once referred to generally as the 'Dark Ages', but now less so as a greater understanding emerges through closer and more accurate interpretation of documents and advanced archaeological investigations).

The Normans found a busy port and market town, at risk from Scandinavian predators, and decided to build a fortress. Circa 1069, the foundations for the castle, as ordered by William the Conqueror, were constructed around the remains of the temple. The Roman temple's podium, still existing, was retained as part of the floor. The castle was then erected re-using much material to be found in the vicinity. It was one of the first built in England and its keep is the largest, the dimensions determined by the remaining Temple of Claudius foundations. At around 1076 its completion predates the White Tower at the Tower of London.

Peter Froste's © conjecture of Norman Colchester, courtesy Colchester Archaeological Trust

Throughout the Middle Ages the castle and much surrounding land, especially to the north and to the east, was held by the Crown and may have been sparsely occupied. The castle fell into ruin from the C15th, but was used for many years as a prison. In 1645 Matthew Hopkins, the 'Witchfinder General' used the castle to imprison and question suspected witches.

Although there was a threat from King Cnut of Denmark and later, in 1216, from King John, the castle saw comparatively little military action in its lifetime and it is still relatively well-preserved. The remains of the Temple of Claudius below the castle may be seen as part of a guided tour.

The substantial remains of Colchester's castle keep in 1791

2
C13th to C16th • The Franciscan Friars

The use of the area to the north and east of the castle (inside and outside the walls) is likely to have been closely related to its royal ownership. It remained reasonably undeveloped and was perfectly suited for its later purpose when a large rectangular plot became the site of a house of the Franciscan Order. The area to the west later became known as Castle Fields. The area between the present Grey Friars building and the north section of town wall (now Castle and Roman Roads) was later known as Priory Fields. The Grey Friars received many gifts and favours from kings and those with royal connections.

St Francis   Grey Friars   Canterbury Grey Friars – remaining building – similar to Colchester?

The Grey Friars   St. Francis was born at Assisi in 1182. Following a comfortable childhood, he rejected his inherited wealth and committed himself to God. He lived a very simple life of poverty and, in so doing, gained a reputation for being the friend of animals. He established the rule of St. Francis, which became the Order of St. Francis, or the Franciscans (also the Friars Minor) - the Grey Friars - as signified by the colour of their robes (the knots in their white cord represented their three vows). Agnellus of Pisa and eight companions arrived at Dover in 1224 to introduce Grey Friars to England. Franciscans took vows of poverty, chastity and obedience, depending on charity for their livelihood. Their apostolate (active responsibilities) covered pastoral work, preaching, confessions, counselling, social work, missions of peace, welfare of the sick and provision of guest accommodation for pilgrims.

Education was also very important to them. Studies were organised in each district. All students who qualified were then sent to Oxford or Cambridge.

By 1237 Henry III had granted Colchester's Grey Friars some land and they established themselves in an area that is likely to have been part of the castle estate – the Royal Demesne. Ten years later, he gave them 10 marks cash and in 1260 sent 1,000 herrings "to the Franciscans of Colchester". In 1269 he gave them seven oaks "to build their church" and in 1279 granted permission to construct a conduit for a water supply "to the Grey Friars' house" across the king's land and under the town wall to a well granted to them by Nicholas de la Warde. It must have been a considerable project as the friars' complex of buildings would surely have been near to the main road (now High Street) to provide accessibility for the populace.

A controversy of some significance involved the Grey Friars in the mid-1300s. Lionel de Bradenham, lord of the manor of Langenhoe, was steward of Lord Fitzwalter's manor of Lexden. With something of a reputation as a robber-baron he was said to have laid siege to Colchester (threatening to burn the town) in a dispute with Commissioners over fishing rights on the Colne, lasting three months in 1350. There were further misdemeanours, one involving releasing criminals from Colchester castle, and, after his own imprisonment, his breaking out and escaping "to the church of the Friars Minor of the same town". The friars would have been in a difficult position – obliged to offer sanctuary, yet surely well aware they were harbouring and aiding a person of doubtful morals. Amazingly, the Patent Roll (official national administrative record) of 1364 records that "The king of special grace has pardoned him the king's suit touching the said seditions, felonies, and acknowledgement and consequent outlawries." So he appears to have got away lightly. One must wonder how, why and through whose offices.

The C14th saw the friars' presence consolidated and records show continued patronage of various monarchs as well as the support and involvement of local people. In 1306 Edward I gave them six oaks. In 1309, Robert Baron Fitzwalter, Lord of Lexden, gave a foundation (a form of grant or donation, sometimes for a particular purpose) and in 1325 he entered the order – just before his death, as was sometimes the practice amongst wealthy people.

In 1325 Edward II gave the friars a further 4.5 acres; then another half-acre. In 1338 John Caproun gave a plot of land. In 1348 they acquired from John le Porcherde a rood (quarter acre) of land 'for enlargement of their dwelling place'. Sir John Gurnon and his wife Margaret were buried in the Friars' church in 1380. The Friars continued to receive local support with twenty bequests from townsmen in the late C14[th] and C15[th] and in 1422 John Pod gave the friars a further 8.5 acres. With these gifts of land, the friars' estate eventually filled the area bounded by the town wall to the north and east, and their own boundaries to the west (separating them from the castle fields) and to the south (along the main road to East Gate). It is possible, as these amounts apparently total in excess of the extent of the site shown on maps, that they also occupied land beyond the walls. There appears to have been a minor conflict with neighbours in 1428 as the owner of a house adjoining their land was forbidden to place his timbers on the friars' wall. In 1469 King Edward IV granted the friars 52 loads of underwood from his local lands (probably covering and extending well beyond today's High Woods area).

As the C15th progressed the area was beginning to be developed in various ways by different people and in 1478 the Castle Field was encroached upon for gardens. Gifts to the friars continued. In 1516 John Garrington of Munton "bequeaths 10/- (ten shillings) to sing a Dirge (Matins from the Office for the Dead) and Mass for his soul a month after his death". Another recorded gift was in 1518 from Thomas Paycocke of Coggeshall: "To the Greyfriars of Colchester and the Friars of Maldon, Chelmsford and Sudbury 10/- for a trental and 3/4d to repair their houses". A trental is a set of thirty requiem masses, offered for souls of the dead. In 1533 Alice Cawston of Tollesbury gave "20/- to pray for my soul and all Christian souls".

Guardians (heads of Franciscan priories entrusted with charge/care of the brothers were so named instead of the normal title of Prior) included John Reylegh in 1419, Walter Bradenham (1458 & 1464) Robert Wotton (1469), Richard (no surname recorded) in 1471, Thomas Lexden (1475) Robert Howell (1482) John Tynemouth, also known as John Maynelyn, (1493) and John Gurdon (1536). Some local place/road names will be recognised here.

John Ashdown-Hill reports that there are also some records of a number of C15th friars: William Sent and Robert Trumpyngton (1435-47), John Horkeslegh (1464), John Bonefaunt (1466/7) and Friar Stokes (1481). He may also have identified a connection between Grey Friars and John Howard (Duke of Norfolk). "The activities which took place in his private chapel may also give some indication of his personal religious commitment. Howard may have had such a private chapel at Tendring Hall in the 1460s, for in 1463 he borrowed 'a pair of organs' from the Greyfriars at Christmas." It is not certain that the friars were the Colchester brothers, but they were very local, so it was likely – even though mediaeval organs were relatively small and portable.

In a study of early C15th Colchester, Richard Britnell comments on literacy and religion. "In 1412 parish organisation gave only minor responsibilities to laymen. The duties of churchwardens required little personal initiative. But literacy was sufficiently widespread to encourage some independence of thought and action in matters of religion. The sons of merchants and other wealthier residents of the town were taught by the master of Colchester grammar school ... Poorer men sometimes learned to read English, at least, without a school education of this kind. There were Franciscans from the house in Friar Street who were willing to help small groups of people wanting to read devotional literature in the mother tongue." 500 years later, literacy teaching in small groups was to return through the adult education service and ended only recently when Essex County Council vacated the site.

The Boundary Walls   We know that the north and east boundary walls of the friary were formed by the town walls. The precise whereabouts of the western and southern boundaries pose more of a problem, however. Although there is currently a substantial wall running north from behind the present Grey Friars building, all the way to the northern section of the town wall, we cannot be certain that this is on the line of the actual friary boundary. This wall contains much re-used material such as Roman tile, dressed stone and some very old brick, but also has 'modern' brick (mostly Victorian), especially where strengthened. It may be that this boundary originated in the C18th, during the considerable tidying-up of the site and was upgraded in the C19th, during the establishment of botanic gardens on the site.

There is an intriguing doorway, below left, currently used as the entrance to a storeroom built against the other side of the wall. This may relate to an C18th right-of-way through Hillcrest. Along the wall there are features resembling niches (such as used to house holy statues) probably erected by the convent and school of the Sisters of Nazareth in the early C20th.

Sections of current boundary wall viewed from Grey Friars side (LPP) and (right) from the Castle Park side adjacent Duncan's Gate

John Speed's map of Essex in 1610 has an inset devoted to Colchester. It has the wrong name (black-cloaked friars were Dominicans), but includes some interesting detail, such as the gateway and the unusual wall alignment next to East Gate near St James' church (see detail below). The front (southern) boundary wall appears to extend into the main roadway, towards the gate and St James's. The line of the site's western boundary is shown on many other maps and especially in the 'North Prospect' in Morant's History of 1748.

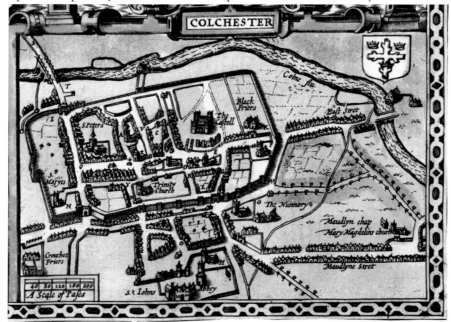

John Speed's C17th map of Colchester, showing Grey Friars boundaries (wrongly named as Black Friars).

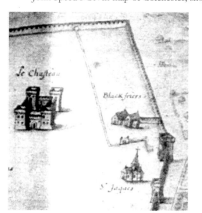

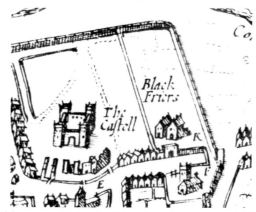

(left) Detail from an undated early map of Colchester   (right) Detail from John Speed's map of 1610

The unidentified early map (left) shows no roads, but some intriguing southern boundary arrangements, as well as buildings, and a gateway, quite near the site of the present house. The town wall's East Gate appears to have a quite substantial building of some kind on its site, depicted on both maps.

Not much is known about the precise position and layout of the friary buildings. Various documents held in the Essex and Public Record Offices give small clues and these include of course these fascinating, but not wholly reliable, maps. From these we can surmise, however, that there was an entrance through a gatehouse in Friar Street (High Street), which seems to have still been in existence in some form in 1622. The main range of buildings was probably set back some distance from the present line of buildings along the main street. Within the friary site, maps show two lines of buildings running parallel to each other, but there is no real evidence of what they were.

If the early maps are at all accurate, it is possible that the original southern boundary of the friary ran along the line of the rear wall of the present Grey Friars and All Saints houses and turned towards the main road just before the East Gate in the vicinity of the modern Roman Road junction with East Hill.

There are some fascinating fragments of an ancient wall to be seen (below) in the construction of the rear outbuildings. This line is followed by the modern (replacement) wall on the boundary of the garden of All Saints House. Again, if it is in a long-established position, this may explain the changing line of the southern boundary near East Gate shown in earlier C16th and C17th maps.

(above right) Modern wall built over pre-existing much older wall on All Saints' boundary (LPP)
(above left & centre) Older wall possibly incorporated in outbuildings at rear of Grey Friars (LPP)

In 'Mediaeval Colchester's Lost Landmarks', Dr John Ashdown-Hill says, "Unlike St Botolph's Priory, the Priory of the Franciscan (or Grey) friars is among the most completely lost of all the great landmarks of mediaeval Colchester. Even if they realise the significance of the name most modern Colcestrians probably have little idea what this building might once have looked like. Today it requires a considerable effort of the imagination to visualise, on the site at the top of East Hill, the very large priory church which once stood there crowned with an octagonal belfry and a tall, slender spire. Nevertheless, thanks partly to its impressive site on elevated ground dominating the eastern approaches to the town, this forgotten building must once have been the most notable of Colchester's landmarks. Its tall spire would have been a feature visible for miles around, rather like the clocktower of the town hall is today. Neither St Botolph's Priory (on its low-lying site) nor St John's Abbey (situated off to one side of the town and partly hidden behind the town walls and its own precinct walls) can possibly have rivalled the visual impact of the Franciscan Priory Church, which, in the later Middle Ages, must have been by far the most prominent feature on Colchester's skyline."

John Ashdown-Hill's © conjecture of the Colchester Franciscan Friary church, seen from the south (Frere Street, now High Street)

Other Grey Friars sites   As we have no above-ground remains of the friary buildings, and only a limited range of documentary evidence of what they may have looked like, it is necessary to use evidence available on the sites of other Franciscan houses as a guide to what may have been here.

The remaining church tower of the Grey Friars, Kings Lynn, Norfolk (below) gives an indication as to what the pattern of building may have been, as does the conjectural drawing (below, left) of the Grey Friars in Newgate, London.

Grey Friars Tower (minus its spire), Kings Lynn, Norfolk

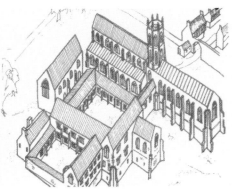

(left) Grey Friars, London, conjecture by H.W.Brewer 1895
(right) Walsingham Grey Friars – adjusted to represent probable Colchester Grey Friars layout –
gateway to High Street would be across top right-hand corner - courtesy John Ashdown-Hill ©

Colchester's premises, although similar in layout, including buildings for all main functions, would not necessarily have been on the same scale as others.

St James' church   Close by Grey Friars, on the opposite side of the street, at the top of East Hill, is the church of St James the Great. It stands in a prominent position, on the crest of the rise, just inside the town wall, near to the site of the Roman East Gate. Parts of the building display architecture of the period around the late C12th and early C13th, with a considerable amount of C14th building in the tower. The main part of the church is reported to have been rebuilt in the C15th. It suffered various periods of decay in the C17th and C19th, spending some time out of commission. Pevsner described the building as the best perpendicular work in Colchester.

Engraving depicting St James' church and the crest of East Hill circa 1824

Whatever the precise date of its first construction may be, it was certainly around in one form or another at the time that the Grey Friars began to set up their own living quarters and church, raising the possibility of some interaction between the two religious sites. But, the church's website states that it was St Botolph's priory, one of the first Augustinian priories in the country, which was the patron in the C14th and possibly earlier. No significant connection with Grey Friars has otherwise been identified to date.

The history of this church is rich in religious and social significance, both locally and nationally, not least for its connection with the radical John Ball.

It is reported that John Ball came to Colchester to be the rector of St James' and became very popular with local villeins (peasant / tenant farmers legally tied to a lord of the manor). He was famous for his anti-establishment sermons, including "When Adam delved and Eve span, who was then the gentleman? From the beginning all men by nature were created alike, and our bondage or servitude came in by the unjust oppression of naughty men." Such egalitarian speeches fuelled the Peasants' Revolt, so it was not surprising that Ball was driven out of the established church and resorted to preaching in streets and churchyards. Eventually being imprisoned, he was freed by Wat Tyler's peasant rebels, but was eventually hung, drawn and quartered in 1381.

The St James the Great church building features as a landmark on many of the drawings depicting the area in the C17th/18th and serves to locate the various parts of the Grey Friars site in its progressive stages of development in maps and diagrams drawn up over the centuries.

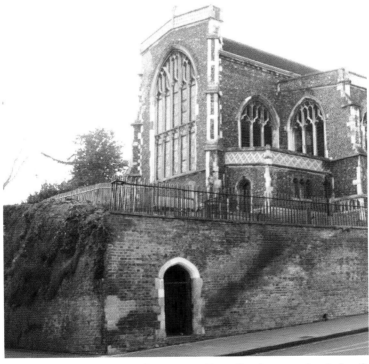

The site of the Roman wall and its East Gate lies just to the left of the high wall of the churchyard, bottom left in the above photograph (see also p28).

3
C16th to C17th • Breakup and Decay

Dissolution of the Monasteries   In 1534 Henry VIII declared himself supreme head of the Church in England in place of the Pope. By 1535, on his behalf, Thomas Cromwell (First Earl of Essex and Lord Great Chamberlain) had ordered the valuation of church property prior to closure of the monasteries, starting with the smallest, circa 1536. Last to go was Waltham Abbey on 23rd March 1540. Controversy between church and state had gripped all concerned and in 1534 local priests were heavily involved. Dr Thyrstell of Grey Friars and neighbour John Wayne, Rector of St James's are reported to have urged local people to ignore new books 'of the King's print'.

The Colchester friary was dissolved in 1538. Much of the valuable material was plundered, but most buildings remained in some form, although the monarch reserved the right to dismantle and remove any structure. The Crown first leased the defunct Grey Friars premises to Francis Jobson, farmer, for £2/10s/8d and then in 1544 granted some of it (listed as *"le olde halle, le fermerye house, Syr Thomas Tyrrells lodgynge chambers, the kitchen, the bakehouse, the brewhouse, two little gardens and four acres of land"*) to Francis and Elizabeth Jobson, Robert Henage, Richard Duke and their heirs. Other changes of ownership followed in 1565 and 1595.

The Tyrrell family's very close connection with Grey Friars is apparent in the will of Sir Robert Tyrrell, written in 1507. *"First I give my soul to Almighty God ... my body to be buried within the church of the Greyfriars of Colchester by Dame Christian, my wife ... also I will that the said friars shall have paid by th' hands of mine executors ... 5 marks yearly sterlings conditionally that the warden ... shall appoint a friar, a brother of the same convent, to sing for my soul and my said late wife soul and for those souls that I am most bound to do for ... "*

And in a definite and precise reference to the Grey Friars premises he states *"Item, I will that mine executors shall make an arch of freestone in the wall within Our Lady's Chapel thereas I and my last wife shall lie, and also I will have a stone of marble to be laid on me and my wife in the said place over our grave, and a*

24

remembrance of my name and hers in the said marble stone ... " Thomas Tyrrell is mentioned in the will as "*mine eldest son.*"

Francis Jobson's success in securing a lease to farm part of the Grey Friars site seems to have been at the expense of a claim by Sir John Rainsford, who was parliamentary representative for Colchester (along with Richard Rich, with whom he had an awkward relationship at times). He was apparently appointed more from his connections in the county and at royal court than local significance and support. Indeed, he appears to have been something of a difficult character, for his style and manner in staking a claim for a share in the distribution of the Grey Friars site after the dissolution seems to have resulted in a firm refusal. Thomas Cromwell rebuffed him, preferring to give Francis Jobson use of the land.

Civil War   One of the most significant events during the C17th was the Siege of Colchester, when Royalist troops supporting King Charles I sought refuge within the town walls and were besieged by the Parliamentary forces of Sir Thomas Fairfax, supporting Oliver Cromwell's cause.

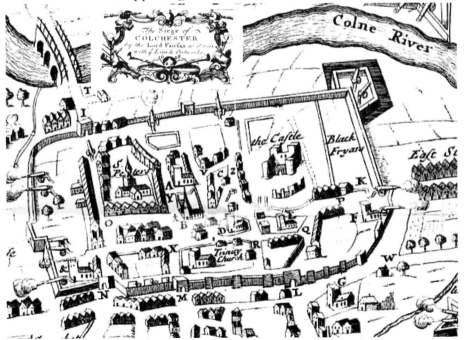

"The Siege of Colchester By the Lord Fairfax, As it was with ye Line and Outworks 1648" (detail showing the walled town)

The town's citizens were caught up in the conflict and suffered starvation, economic disaster and heavy fines for their involvement, albeit mostly involuntary.

Grey Friars is mentioned in the agreement governing the conduct of the surrender on 27th August 1648: *"That all private soldiers and officers under Captains, shall be drawn together into the Fryar's Yard adjoyning to ye East Gate, by 10 of the clock to-morrow morning, with their cloths and Baggage; their persons be rendered into ye Custody of such as the Lord General shall appoint to take the charge of them, and that they shall have faire quarter, (according to the explanation, made in the answers to ye first quarre* [query] *of the Coms* [Commissioners?] *from Colchester, which is hereunto annexed)."* The 'first query', "What is meant by rendering mercy?" was answered as follows: "By fair quarter we understand, that with fair quarter, for their lives, they shall be free from wounding or beating, shall enjoy warm clothes to cover them, and keep them warm, shall be maintained with victuals fit for prisoners, whilst they shall be kept prisoners."

It will be noted that in the closer detail from the siege map (above) the Grey Friars site is still mistakenly labelled "Black Fryars" as the diagram was probably based on Speed's original map.
'K' marks the Friars' yard, now approximately where Roman Road meets East Hill.

Again, we have the same intriguing front boundary line seen in earlier maps. Such an arrangement, which may have something to do with the remains of the Roman eastern gate and guardhouse, could indeed have formed what may be termed 'the friars' yard'. This was, of course, only a convenient name, for the friars were long gone by this time.

In this drawing of 1697, a building within the site can be seen, as can a twin-gabled building along the High Street frontage. A western wall is also in evidence. The enlargement below shows this more clearly. Note also the western wall's diversion to the right (westwards), apparent in other views.

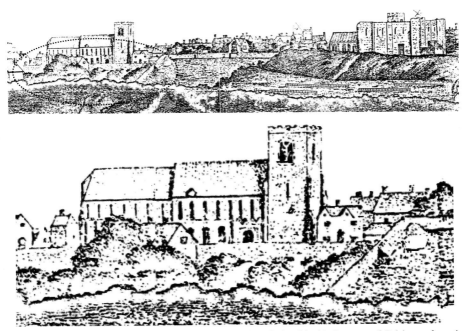

The Castle area and Grey Friars site (top, within dotted oval) is depicted in this Prospect of Colchester from the North 1697 by James Maheux (redrawn and held in the British Library).

The nearby East Gate was badly damaged during the siege. In 1772 Daniel Defoe observed that Colchester "still mourns in the ruins of a civil war" with "battered walls, breaches in the turrets and ruined churches". There seems to have been a general aura of decline in the neighbourhood during the C17th. Part of the East Gate fell down in the 1650s before being removed in 1675 and in 1676 there was further demolition due to the wall's instability in that area. However, part of the Roman guard house (it is not clear what and how much) was reputed to be still in evidence in 1813 (with some evidence in a sketch by John Constable), but was cleared away later in a further tidying-up exercise circa 1819. Constable's drawing (below) shows the remains in 1813. No 1 East Hill is on the left, St James' church eastern end is visible, with its boundary wall on the slope (next to the person walking downhill) and the remnants of East Gate between the house and churchyard wall, where there is now an entrance way to modern buildings set back from the main road.

Drawing by John Constable of the south side of East Gate, Colchester 1813 courtesy Victoria and Albert Museum ©

The East Gate is believed to have had a central road, two pedestrian archways (as Balkerne Gate) and a guard house.

4
C18th • Gradual Regeneration

In the period circa 1700 the Grey Friars site's previous complicated ownership and tenancy arrangements seem to have continued. Various deeds in the Essex Record Office show that a Suffolk man, Thomas Carpenter, passed the estate to his grandson Thomas Bayes (born to Carpenter's daughter Ann, who married Joseph Bayes of an Ipswich ship-building family).

In the period to 1740 a number of people are mentioned in various legal documents concerning leases (Thomas Carpenter, John Eagleton, Ann and Joseph Bayes, Mary Carpenter and Nathaniel Carpenter) but it is not clear who actually occupied which part of the property, if any. Between 1740 and 1751 various arrangements seem to have taken place between Samuel Bayes and Dr Robert Potter, whose heirs in 1752 appear to have sold the whole estate to Rev John Halls. Around this period the remaining ruins of the friary (the only available depiction of which is shown below) were swept away.

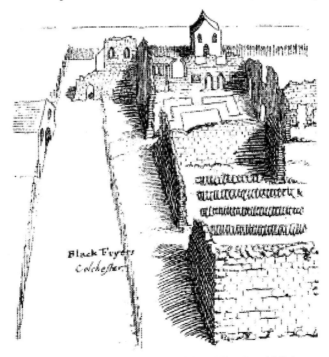

Drawing of part of the site by William Stukely 1718 (Essex Record Office)

Georgian elegance   The period 1714 to 1830 was characterised in England by marked cultural awareness, industrial growth and urban development. Colchester, although not at the forefront of industrial and economic change, remained an important centre for north Essex and south Suffolk and many wealthy men established impressive town houses during this period. There was a confidence in the town at this time and many improvements took place. William Stukeley's drawing of 1718 shows the remaining friary buildings before the tidying-up of the Georgian period transformed this part of town into a very desirable area. Unfortunately it gives no information on the orientation of the view, although in terms of his access, he may be likely to have drawn it from the south, looking north. Stukely also drew the St Botolphs Priory ruins, which themselves had a Grey Friars connection through ownership by the Selley and Halls families.

The new buildings about to arrive in this part of town would give the area an air of elegance worthy of its new residents. The Grey Friars site's prominent setting would now come to the fore in providing dignified residences for leading citizens.

The commanding views afforded by the elevated position along the eastern end of High Street (previously known as Frere Street) made the area a highly desirable location for magnificent houses of local gentlemen. Holly Trees, East Hill House, the remodelled Minories and, of course, Grey Friars (in its superior position) are perfect examples.

Current view from Grey Friars, over roofs of Roman/Castle roads towards High Woods (LPP)

30

Much later, in 1941, Eric Rudsdale (museum curator) would allude to this setting in his diary of the Second World War. *"From my office window at Holly Trees: Green grass of the Park lawns, green leaves of the ancient trees on the Ramparts, russet and yellow flowers in the beds beneath the windows. Pale green of the distant meadows at Mile End Hall, olive green of High Woods beyond them. The sky is a blue vault, with a few fleecy clouds and the brazen sun beating down. Over everything, the brooding lazy heat. No wind, the trees hardly moving in the still, hot air, the distant woods fading in a haze."*

Such must have been the prospect from upper storeys at Grey Friars. It is no wonder that the site was chosen as the setting for an elegant house.

Georgian Colchester   The prosperity of Georgian Colchester, the largest town in Essex, was founded largely on wealth accumulated during the previous centuries' cloth trade. Most of the larger, more impressive houses in the town were built by an elite group of families. Hollytrees was built in 1716 and inherited by the widowed Sarah Creffield, whose second husband, Colchester MP Charles Gray, built the west wing and landscaped the castle grounds.

Opposite Grey Friars, East Hill House, built circa 1740 by George Wegg, is one of the finest and is listed as Grade I owing to its importance. Elsewhere, in the centre of town in West Stockwell Street, Dr Richard Daniell built St Martin's House, thought to have been designed by James Deane circa 1734 similar to Grey Friars. The Rebow family house (home of a Colchester MP), although much altered, still stands at Headgate (corner of Sir Isaac's Walk). There is a Grey Friars connection here, for Sir Isaac Rebow's first wife (circa 1682) was Mary, daughter of James Lemyng of Grey Friars.

The period 1714 to 1830 (the reign of four Georges) was certainly a time of improvement in the street scene in Colchester. English society was going through great change in taste, highly influenced by the 'grand tour' of Europe undertaken by those who were both wealthy and educated. In architecture especially, following Robert Adam's own 'grand tour', fashion brought the 'Palladian' movement to the fore, following the Renaissance architect Andrea Palladio, whose work was based on ancient Rome's buildings. The best Georgian houses exhibited balanced proportions, high quality and elegance.

Pryer, "A New and Exact Prospect of Colchester taken from ye North Part 1724"   Print available in the British Library

This view (above) of the site in 1724 by Pryer (detail below) shows little change since the 1697 drawing. This and the earlier maps suggest that the building shown along the street frontage, opposite St James' church, is on or near the site of the original gatehouse and the current range of buildings. The building within the site has long gone and may be in the position of the C13th friary structures.

The following view by James Deane, from Morant's book (1748), again shows (circled) the former friary land clearly enclosed, and what may be the remaining (possibly derelict) friary buildings, or other structures in their position, along with other constructions opposite St James' Church.

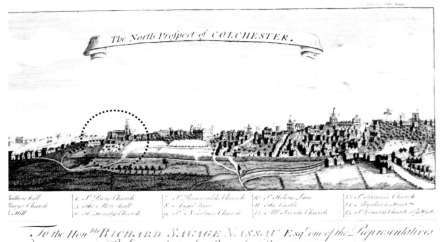

The plate which appears in Philip Morant's "History and Antiquities of Colchester" of 1748 (Grey Friars site circled)

Detail, showing St James' church and the Grey Friars site in front of it, with the appearance of another structure in the intervening 20 years – could this be an earlier, simpler, C18th Grey Friars house, predating Halls' 1755 building?

Twenty-six years after Pryer's view, there appears little change, apart from an additional and separate structure opposite the church. As this is at the time of Dr Potter's tenure, could this be an original C18th house, later to be upgraded in 1755 by Rev Halls, or demolished and replaced entirely? Again, it is situated approximately in the position of the current existing range of buildings.

Also, a slight but distinct curve of the western boundary is still apparent. This is interesting in the context of the present property where the perimeter takes a diversion to the west on reaching the present Grey Friars building, before proceeding south to the High Street. Although the line of the current modern boundary is sharply delineated, with right-angled turns, it may still have something akin to the original northern and southern starting points (ie starting at the town wall, near Duncan's Gate, and ending somewhere along the High Street, near Hillcrest and Winsley's House). The open aspect and commanding position of the site is clear from these C18th views, demonstrating why the location is so special.

Rev John Halls   Rev John Halls (the Rector of Easthorpe) purchased Grey Friars from Dr Robert Potter's heirs in 1752. It is not clear whether he originally purchased an earlier, smaller, simpler house, but it is evident that he is responsible for the current impressive core building of 1755 and 1780.

John Halls joined a rich and interesting family when he married the wealthy Elizabeth Selly of Colchester in 1747. Her mother, also Elizabeth, was a widow who carried on the family brewing business in St Botolph's Street (on the site of the Priory, which she bequeathed to Halls) until her death in 1768. She also owned and bequeathed to Halls the Castle Inn, at North Bridge.

The Castle Inn, North Station Road, now the Riverside Hotel

She must have been a formidable personality. She was apparently the only local landowner not to cave in to pressure over common land use in 1753. Further research may reveal whether Halls was risking his credibility by associating with this family. Quite what his reputation was at the time, however, is not clear as it is possible that his parishioners rarely saw him. It was not uncommon for rectors to have more than one parish and pay a curate to keep them whilst still gathering the stipend. However, upon his death in 1795 the Ipswich Journal did state " … died aged 87 Rev John Halls, a most benevolent and respected character … 60 years Rector of Easthorpe."

Chapman and Andre's map of 1777 (below) shows no sign of any derelict friary buildings. Indeed, no buildings at all are shown apart from along the Frere St (High St) frontage (centre right). There is no sign of the southern wall which ran parallel to, and then turned towards, the main road near to the East Gate. The whole site looks suspiciously tidy, probably owing to the cartographer's simplification of the scene.

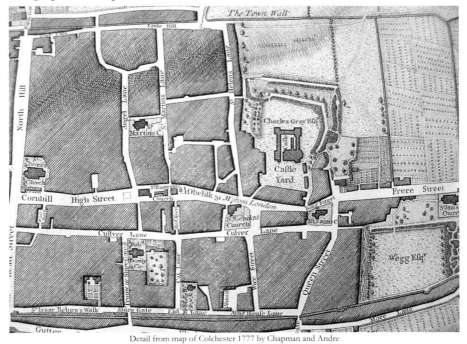

Detail from map of Colchester 1777 by Chapman and Andre

The Castle Fields area (behind and around the castle) remains pleasantly open and undeveloped although there is some encroachment in the south-east

35

quarter along the High/Frere Street (west of Grey Friars). To the south, opposite Grey Friars, the extensive gardens of East Hill House (marked 'Wegg Esq') are within the curve of the Roman wall along More Lane (now Priory Street). It can also be observed how this corner of town contrasts most favourably with much other space within the walls, where although not necessarily totally built-up, it would have been substantially enclosed.

Halls spent a great deal of money on Grey Friars and is responsible for the high quality still apparent today. Halls' nephew, James, of London, owned the house afterwards, but leased it out until its eventual sale to Thomas Baskerfield circa 1814. Baskerfield's widow, Sophie, later passed it to Horatio Cock ('apothecary & physick'). Dr Cock (who married Susanna Round of Birch Hall in 1787) is reputed to be one of eight men who raised funds for Colchester Military Hospital in 1818, was a co-founder of the Essex and Colchester Hospital, and donated staff an 'electrifying machine' in 1826.

Grey Friars' neighbouring C18th buildings   The most important building to appear on the site during the C18th is without doubt the present 'Grey Friars' – the house of 1755 (extended in 1780) at the core of the current complex. But what of the other buildings nearby?

Between Cowdray Crescent and East Hill there is an impressive array of C16th to C18th town houses. Hillcrest, immediately west of Grey Friars, and now attached, is described in its listing (Grade II) as late C18th. Not a great deal is known about this house, but it may have a very close connection with one of the owners of Grey Friars. This is suggested by the presence of a right-of-way leading from the street to the rear of Grey Friars. What is intriguing is that it not only runs alongside Hillcrest ('Lot 3' on the plan below), but through the house! The central diagram (1878) shows a passage through the building, across the back of Grey Friars' side garden, and into the grounds.

 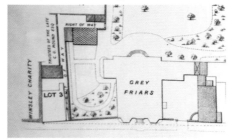 

(above, left) Hillcrest as it is today.   (far right) Hillcrest circa 1900, showing (next to the front door) the entrance to the passageway.

A later plan, drawn in preparation for the conversion of the buildings to a convent and school, shows the right-of-way through Hillcrest being incorporated into the new west wing extension to Grey Friars. The yellow arrow shows the former High Street entrance and the white arrow shows where the right-of-way exited into the Grey Friars garden.

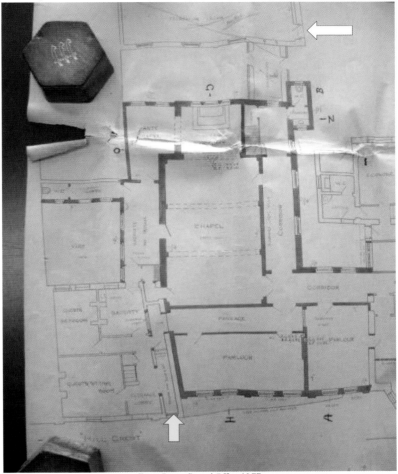

Essex County Record Office / LPP

All Saints House, to the east of Grey Friars, is described in its Grade II listing as C18th with a later C18th front block. The original building of All Saints House is unusual inasmuch as it faces in a different direction from all the surrounding buildings.

The aerial view, below left, clearly shows the original building (facing east, down East Hill – towards the right in the picture) and the addition of the rather unsympathetic extension block which faces the High Street.

Aerial view of All Saints House, 1990s

Late C18th High Street frontage of All Saints House in 2007

As with Hillcrest, it can be seen from the plan (below) that All Saints House, again, has convoluted boundary arrangements (north and south points arrowed) with Grey Friars. The large yard shown on the plan is the eastern yard of Grey Friars, with access to its carriage house and stables. The smaller yard of All Saints, together with its ancillary spaces, clearly overlaps with Grey Friars' utility areas. Again, this suggests a close relationship between the two properties, with All Saints House perhaps owned by Grey Friars and leased out. This would not have been a surprising development, as this was a prosperous part of town, ripe for development and would make sense for Grey Friars' owner to make the most of his assets, investing for the future.

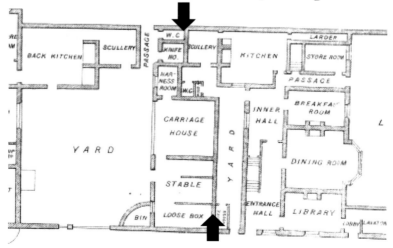

The convoluted boundary between Grey Friars and All Saints, shown by the arrows.

It has been suggested by the Colchester Archaeological Trust that All Saints House may have been built by James Halls Esq., nephew and heir of Rev John Halls. He inherited Grey Friars in 1795 and sold it circa 1814. If this is the case, it may also be James Halls who had Hillcrest built. His ownership spanned sufficient time for him to be able to utilise land either side of the main building, along the street frontage, perhaps in order to maximise his asset in an area of Colchester ripe for development. This would certainly explain the existence of such complicated boundary arrangements – especially if he initially rented out the properties, rather than selling them. Further research may reveal more about this.

Along with All Saints House there is a strip of land along the crest of East Hill, with its substantial boundary wall (seen clearly below). The wall appears to be contemporaneous with the buildings.

All Saints' boundary wall along the High Street / East Hill frontage

(left) Facing south, along the main road (High Street/East Hill   (right) Corner of Roman Road and crest of East Hill

The current boundary walls along Roman and Castle roads are much later than any of the buildings and relate to the enclosure of the current Grey

Friars site in the period following the closure of the Botanic Gardens and development of the residential estate – covered in the next chapter.

The imposing wall to Roman Road – built for privacy after development of the Botanic Gardens for housing?

Former exit to Roman Rd

Roman Rd/East Hill junction

Although the current boundary walls appear very high from the road side, this is partially explained by the difference in ground levels to accommodate roads – as can be seen by the evidence of steps down in the picture (above left).

The northern wall separating All Saints' garden from Grey Friars' garden (right) seems to have been built on much older foundations. There is now an even more modern concrete wall above it, probably built after the Girls' High School vacated the site.

The two other local premises of note, East Hill House and The Minories, both to be found on the opposite side of High Street, are discussed in more detail in Part 2 of this book.

5
C19th • A Desirable Address

The nineteenth century saw Colchester experience further change. Although it remained an important market town for the surrounding rural area, there were economic and social developments which would alter the profile of the town and by 1901 the major sources of employment were the engineering and building sectors, along with transportation of all kinds. These had gradually built up during the C19th, eventually replacing the activities connected to the more traditional trades. For example, business at Grey Friars' owner Stephen Brown's silk factory (built 1824) steadily declined, ceasing by 1881, and its buildings were eventually converted by Truslove's to make steam pumps.

There were major social repercussions to the coming of the garrison in the mid C19th, whose arrival both enriched and challenged the community. Many activities (social, artistic, sporting for example) were enhanced by the presence of all ranks within the military, but there was also drunken and disorderly behaviour and an increase in destitution due to problems with the authorisation process for wives and families to benefit from soldiers' rations.

The development of foundries, engineering firms, quarrying, printing and transport, along with building to cater for the increasing population, was altering the environment. By contrast, this all served to enhance the reputation of the area around Grey Friars as a quiet and fashionable part of town. Although Colchester was not subject to the extremes of social and health problems experienced in the cities (probably due to its slow expansion coupled with its capacity for expansion outwards to accommodate growth) there was inevitably social segregation to some degree.

The leaders of Colchester society in the 19th century included various branches of Grey Friars' neighbours: the Rounds of East Hill House and Hollytrees (they also owned Colchester Castle and Birch Hall) who ranked with the Papillons of Lexden Manor, and the Rebows of Wivenhoe Park. Alongside these locally and nationally powerful dynasties, there were other leading families active in the professions such as doctors, surgeons, clerics and high-ranking military officers. Grey Friars housed examples of all these.

The town's prominent families held on to the more desirable areas such as this site and the owners and occupiers of Grey Friars continued to enjoy a privileged life, exemplified by the following print, showing the view of Grey Friars' 'garden front' across the extensive, elegant and well-tended lawns.

Grey Friars, Colchester.

Print of the Grey Friars gardens and garden front, possibly Victorian era.   Essex County Record Office

It has been suggested that the governors of the Colchester Royal Grammar School considered the Grey Friars site when looking to relocate from their deteriorating premises in the C19th. There is an earlier connection between "the land of the Grey Friars" and this institution through a reference in Colchester Grammar School documents of circa 1540, still to be clarified.

Thomas Baskerfield Circa 1814 Rev John Halls' nephew and heir, James, sold Grey Friars to Baskerfield (1751-1816) a cartographer and topographical artist. Many of his maps are held in the British Library. In 1817 it was willed to Baskerfield's wife Sophia with his executor Horatio Cock and heirs. In 1823 Dr Cock secured the house. In 1824 Priory Field (below the formal gardens) was leased to trustees of the Colchester and Essex Botanical and Horticultural Society. Tenants occupied the house during this time. In 1849 the heirs of Horatio Cock sold the main part of the property (the house - Grey Friars - and its gardens) to Stephen Brown whilst retaining ownership of the land containing the Botanic Garden. Roper's map of 1810 shows a very neatly landscaped area between the house and the town wall to the north. We cannot be sure how accurate this was, especially as he (in common with others) has an incorrect name for the order of friars from which the site takes its name – although it does bear some similarity to the print shown previously. (Crutched Friars, also known as crouched or crossed, carried a staff with a cross/crucifix. They were in Crouch Street, off Lexden Road.)

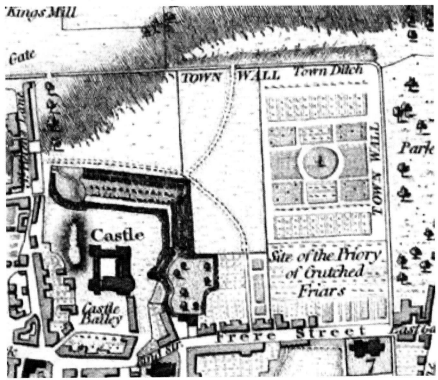

C19th Botanic Gardens   In 1823 the Colchester and Essex Botanical and Horticultural Society was formed and plans were made to establish a facility on 8½ acres of the former friary land, behind the Grey Friars house, leased for 21 years with an option to purchase during that period. Monson's 1848 map (below) shows the site with the Botanic Gardens in situ. Although only showing the main features (pond, perimeter walks, curator's cottage and the entrance path) it gives a clear picture of the extent of the undertaking and how it dwarfs the residential part of the site.

Thomas Cromwell's "History and Description of the Ancient Town and Borough of Colchester, in Essex" (1826) states that "the peculiar feature" of the Colchester and Essex Botanical and Horticultural Society's plan "is the union of a Nursery with a Botanical Garden, through which it is calculated that, in a few years, the profits arising from the former will be fully adequate to the expenses of the latter; when, in consequence, the annual contribution of the proprietors will be no longer required." He also remarks very positively on the area's desirability: "The situation is beautiful, commanding a view of the surrounding country at once varied and extensive; while it is of interest to many, that the ancient wall of the town forms its northern and eastern boundaries."

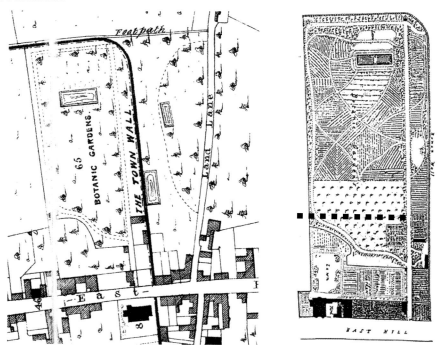

More references to the Botanic Gardens, together with further illustrations, appear in chapter 4 of Part 2 of this book.

On the plan (above, right, circa 1847) the boundary of the Grey Friars house and garden depicted differs from today's northern wall position (shown on the plan as a broken line). As the same convoluted line appears on the original plan for developing Roman and Castle roads this shows that the owner of Grey Friars re-purchased one or more of the lots to square-off his land holding to bring the grounds to their present, almost rectangular, shape.

A great deal of effort went into the planning and operation of the venture. The aims of the Botanical Society were to set out collections of all classes of plants with a classified arrangement for the use of students of botany. Plants would be labelled in English and Latin and it would include fruit trees, shrubs, forest trees and aquatic plants. Cartographical evidence suggests that the large pond in the upper eastern section of the plan of the Botanic Gardens was probably constructed by joining together two original friary fish ponds. Cromwell wrote enthusiastically in 1826: "Considering the limited period that has elapsed since the occupation of this spot, great progress has been made ... It should be mentioned also that there is a fine piece of water, well adapted to the cultivation of aquatic plants ... the walks around which are already in a state of great forwardness, and tastefully disposed. The list of officers will shew that this institution has been highly patronised, and its designs taken up with great spirit; though, like most infant societies, it will require both encouragement and perseverance, ere it can attain its ultimate objects."

Certainly much was done in an attempt to make a success of the Gardens. An 1840 newspaper reports a meeting of the committee where they record gifts such as Rev Mr Holmes of Copford's donation of an assortment of seeds from the Sandwich Islands, commenting "We trust that their example will be followed by others of the nobility and gentry of the neighbourhood, who may possess specimens of curious and rare plants." The committee did its best to encourage use of the gardens. The hours were long (6am to 9pm at peak, although shut on Sundays during Divine Service) and the entrance fee of 2/6d., although very expensive, was refundable if 10/- was spent in the shop.

Attractions included balloon ascents, one recorded in William Wire's diary (see Glossary) for May 17th 1848: *"Mr Green, the celebrated aeronaut, ascended in his balloon from the Botanic Garden about half past three o'clock p.m., and a splendid sight it was, the wind blowing from the south-west with a gentle breeze by which he was wafted gradually to the opposite point of the compass for a short distance, when he began to ascend gradually and was carried to Diss in Norfolk where he descended between five and six o'clock in the evening ... What added to the splendour of the sight was a clear sun, shiny day."*

By 1851, however, the project had failed to reach its potential, there being too few subscribers. The gardens closed and the land was prepared for sale. The National Freehold Land Society, affiliated to the Liberal party, bought them.

Small plots were laid out by T. Morland and C. Wilkinson. Seventy-two lots were bought by builders, craftsmen, merchants, and a few gentlemen. Forty-one were from Colchester, the rest from the London area. The names Castle and Roman Roads were not finally decided upon for ten years and not all of the plots were developed immediately, some being dormant for around forty years. In the 1860s Morland and Wilkinson laid out another small estate west of North Station Road just south of the Eastern Counties asylum consisting of Belle Vue, Colne Bank, and Essex Hall roads.

During the original groundworks for the new houses and roads in 1852 some Roman archaeology was uncovered and subsequent work on alterations and extensions (even ordinary gardening activities) has also produced a variety of finds (some are described in chapter 7 of part 1 of this book).

COLCHESTER AND ESSEX

Botanic and Horticultural Gardens.

Messrs. Shuttleworth and Sons

Have been instructed by the Devisees to SELL by AUCTION, at the Three Cups, Colchester, on TUESDAY, February 11th, at Two for Three in the Afternoon precisely, in numerous Lots, adapted to building operations,

THE reserved portion of the valuable FREEHOLD PRO-PERTY, comprising the important and highly improvable Estate formerly a portion of the Grey Friars, opposite St. James's Church, on East Hill, Colchester, in the County of Essex, approached from East Hill, and bounded on two sides by the ancient town wall, comprising upwards of 8 Acres of LAND, distinguished as the Colchester and Essex Botanic and Horticultural Gardens.

May be viewed with permission of the Tenant; and particulars had of W. R. RIPLEY, Esq., Solicitor, 7, Whitehall Place; at the Three Cups, Colchester; and of Messrs. SHUTTLEWORTH and SONS, 28, Poultry, London.

The original 1852 plan of plots (above, left), shows the proposed, but not implemented, north and south road names Garden Terrace and Rose Terrace. The four plots to the south of "Rose Terrace" (now part of Castle Road) are now incorporated within the boundary of the current Grey Friars complex. The 1851 original sale (press notice, above, right) was arranged in more than

20 lots, but was eventually bought en bloc by the National Freehold Land Society which later became the Abbey National Building Society.

Quaker Burial Ground   By the 1850s the Society of Friends (Quakers) were running out of burial space, so they purchased the four plots on the north-east corner of the site. They used three for burials and reserved one for a cottage, which was never built. They let the plot as a garden, then sold it in 1959. At another time, they bought a further space within the north-east wall and incorporated it with planting and landscaping.

Above (left) Eastern boundary, remains of town wall, looking south (LM)   (right) The entrance gateway in Roman Road

(photo LM)

The picture above shows the remains of the core of the Roman town wall, now forming the north boundary of the Quaker Burial Ground. It once delineated the north-east corner of the original Grey Friars site from the time of the friary, circa 1230s, to the closure of the Botanical Gardens in the 1850s.

47

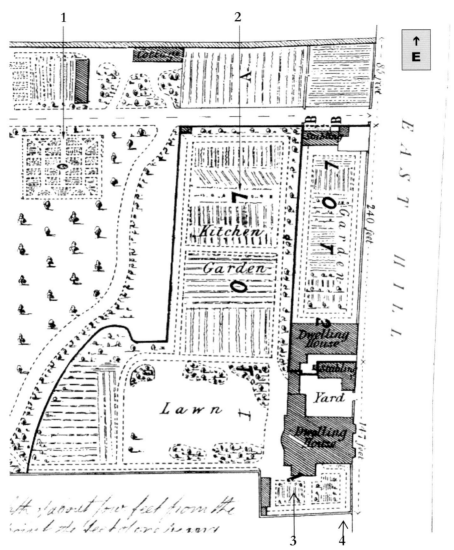

This detail from the sale plan of 1847, shown with north to the left and south to the right, depicts the layout of the Grey Friars and All Saints House premises before the auction.

The number 1 marks the site of the Botanic Garden parterre, which may have been in the vicinity of the location of part of the friars' church; 2 marks the site of the kitchen garden, within which some human burials were discovered; 3 marks the former side garden to the Grey Friars house, now covered by the west wing of 1904; 4 marks the position of Hillcrest, not shown on this plan, which may suggest that it was not included in the sale of 1847. It was, however, added to the current complex when purchased by the nuns who founded a school and convent at Grey Friars in 1904.

Grey Friars and its large gardens form Lot 1. The 'dwelling house' shown as Lot 2 is All Saints House, leased until 1848 to William Waylen Esq and family. He and his brother, who also lived there, were prominent local surgeons.

The entrance pathway (next to the 'E' of East Hill on the plan) is now the corner of Roman Road where it meets East Hill.

Rev John Robert Smythies   This occupant is mentioned in the auction notice issued by Shuttleworth and Sons as being in tenancy at Grey Friars until Michaelmas (September 29th) 1848.

The Smythies family genealogy website describes him as:

"Rev John Robert Smythies B.A. of Grey Friars House, Colchester, and Lynch Court, co. Hereford, Rector of St. Mary Magdalene's, Colchester, etc. Private Chaplain to H.R.H. The Duke of Sussex. One of the founders of the Royal Agricultural Society. b. 1778 – d. 1852"

The portrait is annotated: "From the Miniature in possession of Miss Mary Peachey."

www.smythies.com

Rev John Smythies must certainly have been of strong character. He was involved in some controversy in a debate concerning agricultural matters circa 1823, during which he is reported (www.historyofparliamentonline.org) to have denounced William Cobbett as an "itinerant political tinker". Cobbett (of 'Rural Rides' fame) was a popular journalist, by reputation powerful yet incorruptible, deeply conservative yet keen to embrace advanced political ideas. To some he was a champion of traditional rural England. Smythies was therefore taking on a formidable opponent.

Smythies is mentioned in White's Directory of 1848 as being 'the incumbent of St Mary Magdelen'. It appears that along with this role went some considerable responsibility for a hospital, where it was decreed, after being re-founded by King James I in 1610, "There were to be in it a master, who was to have the cure of souls in the parish of St. Mary Magdalen and to celebrate divine service and preach and administer the sacraments, and five poor persons, each of whom was to receive 52 shillings (£2 12s 0d) yearly at the hands of the master." Successive masters of the hospital viewed this payment to the poor as a fixed sum, and that subject to this payment totalling £13, they were otherwise entitled to keep the whole of the hospital's income to themselves.

To test this, in 1831, the Attorney General filed an action against Smythies, who was then master of the hospital, and the Master of the Rolls declared that the hospital's master was not thus entitled, and that the profit made by the agreement with the Board of Ordnance was to be considered the property of the charity, with the master entitled to the interest only, except for reimbursement of his costs in restoring the lands.

Rev John Smythies appealed to the Lord Chancellor, who in 1833 reversed some aspects, the effect of which was to uphold the right of the master to all revenue subject to the yearly alms payment. The yearly income of the hospital then amounted to £239/5s/0d, besides the dividends on £4,754/3s/7d. The old hospital having become dilapidated, it had been pulled down about six years before this decree, and Smythies had erected on its site six tenements under one roof, adjoining the churchyard of the parish of St. Mary Magdalen, each containing two rooms. One was unoccupied, and the other five were inhabited by five poor widows, to each of whom the master paid the statutory 52 shillings annually. The site, in Brook Street, has a fascinating history and is the subject of an extensive report by the Colchester Archaeological Trust.

Stephen Brown   This notable Grey Friars resident was a silk throwster and magistrate. Born 1800, at Wivenhoe Hall, he married Fanny in 1833.

He secured the Grey Friars house from the family of Horatio Cock in 1849 and by a series of conveyances and covenants between 1849 and 1853, he obtained various 'lots' of the broken-up estate from four other owners, including Mr Thos. Green and Mr and Mrs Atkins, and the developers Messrs

Morland and Wilkinson. This eventually resulted in the basic extent of the present site, within the tall red-brick walls, we now know as Grey Friars.

The census of 1851 shows Stephen (aged 51) living at Grey Friars with his wife Fanny (39), daughters Fanny (17), Martha (15), Anna Victoria (12), Amelia (8), Julia (3) and son Richard (6). There were also five servants: John Catt (a footman), Frances Jones (Nurse), both of Wivenhoe, Lucy Harvey (cook) of Dovercourt and two maids, Anne Gage of Colchester and Harriet Sparrow of Layer Marney. There were different staff listed in 1861. Of the family, Stephen, Fanny and Amelia are listed along with Alice J (13) and Isabella (7). Only Isabella was born at Grey Friars and she also died there in 1869 aged 15. She is buried with her parents at St Mary at the Wall.

Brown was one of the last silk manufacturers in Colchester, with a four-storied factory near the river in what is now St. Peter's Street. This road is interesting for its varied names. Previously it was: (possibly) Fowles Lane, 1330; Dead Lane, 1702, becoming Factory Lane, 1851, after Brown and Moy's silk factory. The precarious nature of Brown's business is referred to in William Wire's diary, February 1843: "Several men were discharged from the silk factory of Brown and Moy, and it is closed two days a week in consequence of the depression of the silk trade." The factory ceased in 1881.

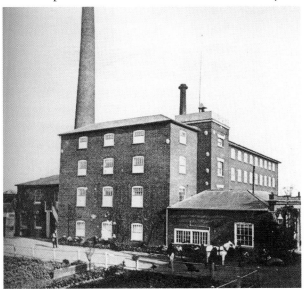

Stephen Brown's silk factory 'Brown and Moy' in 1878 (now demolished) Factory Lane, now St. Peter's Street

51

He also owned a mill in Hadleigh (Suffolk) until about 1853, which had its own gas works and for some time supplied gas to the town. He is reputed to have designed a gas meter, fitted as a trial in Grey Friars, eventually being taken by the erstwhile 'Gas Board' and placed in their museum. Unfortunately, efforts to trace this post-privatisation have failed.

The Brown family would have seen the balloon ascents from the Botanical Gardens in 1851 and witnessed their decline and sale for building land.

Press announcement for the final major event in the history of the Botanic Garden.

MR. C. GREEN
will take his 510th Ascent, from the Lawn,
ON TUESDAY, the 27th day of MAY, 1851,
IN HIS
SPLENDID BALLOON
THE ROYAL VICTORIA AND BRUNSWICK,
which measures 120 feet in circumference, contains 200,000 gallons of Gas, and with the Car attached is 70 feet high, with which he had the honour to convey his Highness the Duke of Brunswick from London to Boulogne, in France, on March 31st, 1851, a feat which no other aeronaut ever could accomplish.

Under the Patronage of the Subscribers to the Garden.

MESSRS. W. & A. BURGESS
RESPECTFULLY inform the Nobility, Gentry, and Inhabitants of Colchester and its Vicinity, that they have engaged Mr. C. GREEN, Aeronaut to the Royal Gardens, Vauxhall, to make ONE GRAND ASCENT from the Lawn of the BOTANIC GARDEN, on TUESDAY, May 27th, 1851, in his magnificent BALLOON the "Royal Victoria and Brunswick," which is formed with 1,200 yards of silk, manufactured for the express purpose, in alternate gores of Crimson and Gold, with a belt, on which is inscribed "Royal Victoria," in gold letters 3 feet high, with crowns and other national emblems.

The Public are particularly solicited to give this Third and Last Balloon Ascent from this Garden their united patronage, which will be esteemed a great favour on the part of Messrs. Burgess.

Garden to be Open at Two o'clock, when partial Ascents will be made; the final Ascent will take place punctually at 5 o'clock.

Admission 1s. each; Children under 12 years and Schools 6d. each.

A GOOD BRASS BAND
has been engaged for the day, and will enliven the scene with a series of popular Airs.

Mr. Forbes, from the George Inn, will supply Refreshments in a good Marquee.

Tickets may be had at the Garden; of Mr. TAYLOR, *Essex Standard* Office; at Mr. BENHAM'S; and at the Cups and George Hotels.

For the accommodation of Ladies a good Booth will be placed on the Lawn.

Subscribers to the Garden will be presented with a Ticket to admit themselves and their immediate Families to witness the Ascent.

All the Charity Schools in Colchester and the Tendring Hundred will be admitted Free, with their Governors and Governesses.

Subscribers and Schools must take their Tickets from the 19th to the 24th instant at the Garden.

The Eastern Counties' Railway will run Trains from Chelmsford, Maldon, Braintree, Witham, Kelvedon, and Mark's Tey, to Colchester and back, at
A SINGLE FARE.

A subsequent newspaper report of the event details the 'disappointing' turnout of only about 1500, supposing that it was due to a combination of the weather and lack of novelty due to previous ascents. The evening entertainment, "a brilliant display of fireworks by Mr Gyngell the celebrated pyrotechnist" was more successful.

Roman Road and Castle Road The development of the land which was once the Botanic Gardens, previously known as Priory Fields, has resulted in some very attractive residential streets, a much sought-after location. The area is rich in history and residents have fascinating stories of previous occupation, cottage industries and interesting artefacts found when digging the gardens.

(above and below) cottage against wall in garden of no 68 Castle Road.

(above) Southern section of Roman Road adjacent East Hill
(below) Castle Rd with Grey Friars' earlier western boundary wall

Another Castle Rd (LM) property with building against the western wall

(above) Castle Road, looking north towards the northern section of town wall. (LPP)
The C18th and C19th western perimeter wall of the Grey Friars site is at the end of the gardens of the houses to the left.

53

(above) Roman Road, east side – a range of architectural styles.
The eastern section of the town wall runs along the rear of the gardens to these properties.

The northern boundary of the Botanic Garden, and before that the Grey Friars estate, and probably the Franciscan Friary boundary.
(above) Roman Road – looking westward, along the remains of the northern section of the town wall.
(inset) The breach in the town wall at the end of Castle Road (LM)

Other residents of Grey Friars   Following the Browns, there was a succession of tenants and owners. There were also some complicated legal arrangements still to be traced, including Hillcrest, involving variously, Richard Durrant, Douglas Round, Rev CF Norman and BH Nicholson.

Captain Fitzroy Wilson   The Post Office Directory of Essex, 1874, shows Wilson resident at 'Grey friars, East Hill' (sic). With not even the Post Office getting the address correct, this illustrates one of the pitfalls in tracing occupancy of premises throughout history. 'Greyfriars', '81 High Street', and simply 'High Street' (with no indication of precise location) have been versions of the address used in various listings.

Sale in 1878   By the time of the 1878 sale, the plan (below) showed that Roman and Castle roads had been well established, with plenty of building having taken place. Also, the shape of the present complex had been adopted and on this occasion Hillcrest was included in the sale.

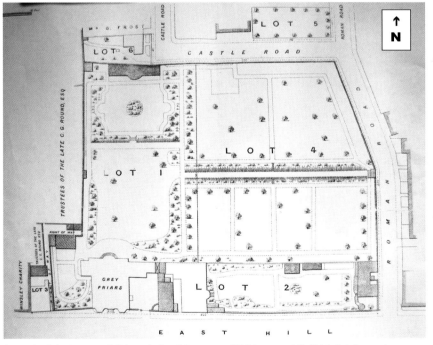

The above plan is by Sexton and Grimwade, Land Surveyors of Colchester and Hadleigh. It is interesting to note that it was possible that the Grey Friars gardens could have been diminished had lot 4 been purchased separately.

55

Major General Radcliffe   The 1881 census shows Grey Friars occupied by 58 year old Radcliffe, his wife (48), son aged 7 and five servants, one of whom was the butler, an 'army pensioner' aged 49; none had local origins.

Rev Canon John Howard Marsden   This distinguished and learned gentleman was born in Wigan in 1803 and educated at Manchester Grammar School and St John's College, Cambridge. He was variously a professor of archaeology at Cambridge, Rural Dean of Harwich, and the writer of various religious, antiquarian and archaeological papers.

He married Caroline, the daughter of Dr Moore of Lincoln Cathedral in 1840. Marsden was a member of the Colchester Castle Book Society, a prestigious group having access to high quality literary and historical material. He was also involved in the formation of Essex Archaeological Society, which started in Colchester. He lived at Grey Friars with his wife and their three sons from 1884 whilst the Rector of Great Oakley, a post he held for 49 years. He died at Grey Friars, in January 1891.

left: Rev J.H. Marsden (Colchester Local Studies Library)
Information and illustration courtesy Dr Michael Leach

Lt Colonel William Marsden   The census of 1891 records occupation by the son of Rev JH Marsden. It shows William Howard Marsden (49, retired from the army), Katherine his wife (32) children William (16), Audrey (15), Wilfred (12), a boarder (a governess from Germany) and five servants, (cook, schoolroom maid, parlour maid, housemaid and kitchen maid) three of whom were local. Shortly afterwards, the house was sold to Dr EL Fenn.

Edward Liveing Fenn MD   In 1891 the "Trustees of the Will of the late Rev. J.H.Marsden" conveyed Grey Friars to Dr Fenn, who, due to ill health, was moving to the cleaner air of Colchester from Richmond, Surrey. Dr Fenn had practised in Richmond for twenty years and was consulting physician to the Royal Richmond Hospital. His first wife Katharine died aged 35 from "chronic inflammation of the lungs". In 1892 he married Edith Todd.

Adria Margaret Fenn, born in 1895 to Dr Fenn's second wife, during the family's time at Grey Friars, wrote in 1962, aged 67: "Father's health not being very good, he resigned from his practice in Richmond soon after his second marriage and went to live at Grey Friars, Colchester. He became consulting physician at Colchester Hospital. I was a very small child at the Colchester house, but I well remember the happy home atmosphere there, with parents devoted to one another, five good-natured big brothers, and 'Beau' a year older than myself to share our nursery. At Colchester, and at Nayland, he organised Shakespeare readings amongst his friends and relations. He was a good amateur actor and recited very well, and loved to recite from the Suffolk Ballads". Adria is pictured below in her early childhood, outside the bay window in the 'garden front', with Edward, born in Grey Friars 1894, sadly dying young, as a Lieutenant, in action in Palestine in September 1918.

(left) Dr Fenn's last two children, Edward Gerald Palmer and Adria Margaret, posing outside the garden front at Grey Friars circa 1900   (right) Family group in Grey Friars western side garden

Letters in the family archive give a glimpse of Colchester gentry's Victorian/Edwardian life. In May 1895, Fenn wrote to his son from his desk at Grey Friars: "… I drove Edgar over to Dedham last Friday in the dogcart and we had tea with Aunt Annie. It was very dusty and windy on the road. As I am writing now in the study the clouds of dust continue to roll by, we very much want some beautiful showers of rain to lay the dust and make the vegetables grow …"   November 1896: "We had our Shakespeare reading party last Thursday the arrangements much the same as we had two years ago. The bow window in the drawing room a bank of flowers for the stage, tea in the study, and supper in the dining room. Everyone said it was a brilliant evening so we were repaid for our trouble." It is still possible to sit in the Grey Friars garden room and imagine this gathering.

Dr E.L. Fenn

The two-page extract (below) from a letter of July 1897 to Ernest Vanderzee (aged 17) in both parents' hands (Dr Fenn – 'Father' and stepmother Edith – 'Mater') gives further insight into family and social life at Grey Friars in the late 1800s. One can picture the scene: "This Thursday we had a garden party – about 35 or 40 people – croquet ... ... ices - & strawberries were the chief attraction with two exceptions – viz Bo & Chick who appeared in white from head to foot - and were much admired."

'Bo' is Edward Gerald Palmer, aged nearly 3 years at the time and 'Chick' is Adria Margaret, aged nearly 2 years. Ernest Vanderzee ('Van') spent a great deal of time away from home at school and university, then, as Rev. E.V. Fenn, joined his brother in New Zealand.

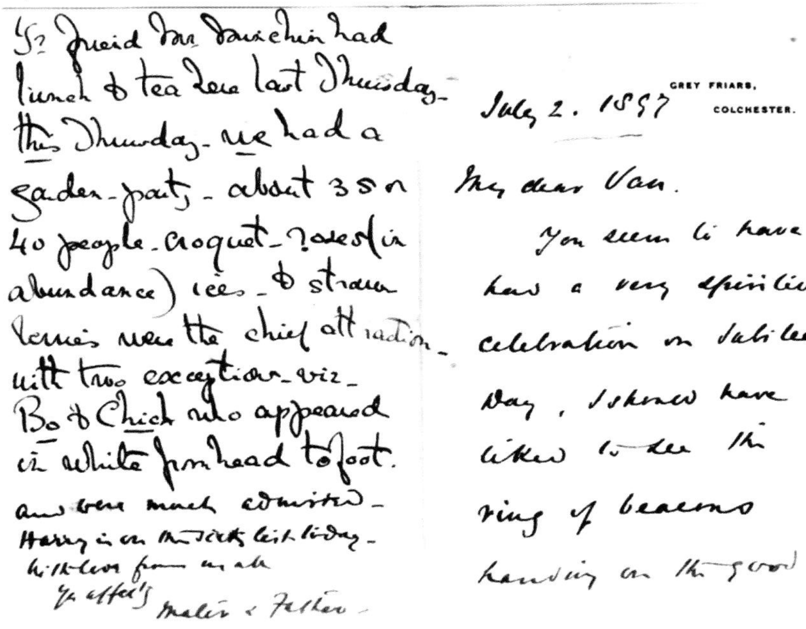

July 2. 1897   GREY FRIARS, COLCHESTER.

[Handwritten letter]

Sr Jneid Mrs Saischin had lunch & tea here last Thursday — this Thursday we had a garden-party — about 35 or 40 people. Croquet — roses in abundance) ices — & straw berries were the chief attraction — with two exception viz — Bo & Chick who appeared in white from head to foot. and were much admired —

Harry is on his sixth birthday — with love from us all Yr affec'y mother & Father —

My dear Van.

You seem to have had a very spirited celebration on Jubilee Day, I should have liked to see the ring of beacons handing on the good

The extensive gardens (even after the loss of many acres in 1824) were clearly a major feature of family life at Grey Friars. Whether used for social gatherings (as referred to in the letter), as a safe playground for the children, or for quiet solitude and contemplation by the adults, they must have been much-loved by the families occupying the premises over the years.

GREY FRIARS FROM GARDEN.   THE GARDEN.

Group at Grey Friars

Fenn family gathering likely to be early in their occupation of Grey Friars. (left to right) Back row: (Dr to be) Charles Edward Fenn (possibly), Dr Edward Liveing Fenn, unknown; third row: (Rev to be) Ernest Vanderzee Fenn, Katherine Mary Hopkins, Cyril Duncan Fenn, (Rev to be) Edgar Julius Fenn, Dorothy E.D.Cotes, Harold Liveing Fenn; second row: Lewis Hopkins, Lucy Vanderzee Hopkins nee Fenn, unknown, Edith Fenn nee Todd (Edward's second wife), Isabella Francis Louisa Cotes nee Fenn. Front row: Rees Hopkins, unknown, unknown.

Harold Fenn (pictured on the next page) wrote from Grey Friars to his brother in February 1897, aged 20: "I like my life at Paxmans very much my daily routine is this I get up at about five or ten to six, begin work at half past, leave off at 8.20 come home for breakfast ... begin again at 9 go on till 1pm and then from 2 till 5.30pm, so I have a good long day of it. I have got a nice bicycle. Lately I have purchased a cyclometer ... Since the beginning of last week up until now I have been 71 miles. When you come home I will take you round the works and show you the molten iron, furnaces etc. Harold L.Fenn PW (Paxmans workman)". Dr Fenn had five sons by his first marriage and, after remarrying, a further son and two daughters, one of whom died aged 6 months. Harold became a mechanical and electrical engineer after training at Davey Paxman and Christy Brothers and Middleton of Chelmsford, one of the pioneers of electrification in the early C20th. He was responsible for installation of steam turbine driven electrical generating plants. For health reasons he emigrated to New Zealand in 1906, a wise move because he lived to be 91. It is his son from whom we have the information.

Dr Fenn's son, Harold Liveing Fenn visiting Grey Friars circa 1900, posing by the garden front of 1780

The 1901 census shows Grey Friars (as 81 High Street) occupied by Edward, a physician/surgeon aged 57 born in Nayland, Edith, his wife aged 43 born in London, son Edward G.P. (6), daughter Adrea M. (5) both born in Colchester and four servants, Florence Kettle (parlour maid, born in Maldon), Edith Lovett (housemaid, Ipswich), Sarah Vyce (cook, Norfolk), Amy Blount (nurse, Worcestershire). This was the last family to live at Grey Friars as their home and it is from them that we have the most evocative view of family life on the site in the early C20th. They lived there for twelve years.

View from upper floor of Grey Friars across the Fenns' tennis court and northward over Castle and Roman roads

(left) Grey Friars servants around the turn of the century   (right) garden scene

Detail from a photograph by Alfred Wire, © Vestry House Museum, London Borough of Waltham Forest

The above photograph shows the east end of High Street and the crest of East Hill in 1903 before the building of the convent school extensions of 1904.

Grey Friars is partially hidden by the enormous tree in the western side garden between Grey Friars and Hillcrest. The coach house and stable block to the east have now been replaced by the school's east wing. The building beyond the stable block is the rather unsympathetic side extension to All Saints House.

Dr Fenn eventually inherited and enthusiastically restored grade 1 Elizabethan property "Grooms", later re-named Alston Court, Nayland in 1902, leaving Grey Friars in 1903 to live there. Among legal papers left by his uncle and aunt he found a document signed by Dr Gilberd, which he presented to the Town Council who hung it near to his portrait in the Moot Hall. William Gilberd, born in Colchester, became physician to Elizabeth I and in his spare time he conducted experiments in magnetism and static electricity, famously publishing his findings.

In February 1903 Grey Friars was sold to 'Madame A. Herbert and Others' on behalf of The Sisters of Nazareth, and a convent with school was established, thus beginning over 100 years of educational activity on the site.

Grey Friars between 1891 and 1903
Images and information in this section courtesy of Fenn family archive: www.thekingscandlesticks.com

When Dr Fenn died in 1907, aged 64, obituaries appeared in many prestigious publications including the British Medical Journal. They celebrated a significant life of achievement professionally, socially and in the community, lived to the full by "a very fine type of man ... unquestionably an honour to his profession ... a dignified gentleman ... universally beloved and esteemed by all who came into contact with him".

6
C20th • The Educational Era

We saw in chapter 2 that Richard Britnell's research on the C15th revealed that the ground-breaking Grey Friars adult literacy programme of the 1980s and 1990s was nothing new after all – it had been preceded 550 years earlier, on the same site, by the Franciscan friars! Ironically, after a gap of 366 years, it was again the Franciscans who brought education back to the site – but this time it was not friars, but nuns. Their arrival began the site's significant school and college era, which was to last for just over 100 years.

Advertisement in the 1908 edition of "The Catholic Who's Who"

Grey Friars Convent In 1903 a group of nuns left France to settle in Colchester and eventually purchased Grey Friars and Hillcrest, contracting local builder Robert Beaumont to join the two houses, build extensions and convert the premises to a convent and school in 1904. It is said that only lay sisters were allowed to leave the building and the only male allowed in was Dr

Nicholson from Gate House, nuns instructing builders through an iron grille. A piscina (holy water basin) and confessional space are still evident in a corridor joining Hillcrest and the school's chapel and assembly hall.

Post card sent in 1906 showing Hillcrest, Grey Friars and the completed extensions. A copy of the same postcard, written in French, was found beneath the floorboards during recent renovations (see Appendix)

The census of 1911, interestingly, shows occupation of both Grey Friars (including Hillcrest) and All Saints House. It states that there are 57 people in residence across 36 rooms occupied in Grey Friars and 8 rooms in All Saints House. Unfortunately it does not differentiate between types of accommodation. The nuns (described as 'inmates') number 25, aged between 27 and 70 years. 15 were French, 5 British, 2 Irish, a Syrian and a Belgian. A further 3 'inmates' are described as teachers and are listed with the schoolchildren. 26 pupils aged 11-18 years were recorded; 12 from France, 11 from England (including three sisters aged 11, 13 and 18) and 3 from Ireland. There were 3 visitors, all single women aged 24, 26 and 35.

When the nuns returned to France in 1920, following a rather troublesome and not very lucrative sale of the premises to Essex County Council, their belongings reputedly filled two barges at the Hythe. There are a number of postcards in existence from this period and many were used by girls writing home (some in French) about their time at the convent school. (Further reference to this is made in Part 2 Chapter 4.)

Could these local sisters be Grey Friars Convent School day girls?

Simon Gallup told us about his aunt (now 100 years old) who, whilst discussing their family, had a recollection that her two older sisters went to school on East Hill and that they were educated by nuns. She was considerably younger than her sisters, who were Beryl Mary Abbott Green, born 1892 and Sybil Mary Abbott Green, born 1894. During the 1901 census they were recorded as living in Fingringhoe. At the time of the opening of the convent school, circa 1904, Beryl would have been 12 years old and Sybil 10, so they would have been of an appropriate age range to be enrolled.

Beryl and Sybil   Beryl in 1911

When the 1911 census was taken, Beryl (19) was at a finishing school in Eastbourne and Sybil (17) was at a boarding school in Windsor. In 1916, Beryl married Colin Morgan Oliver in Fingringhoe. During World War II she worked at Colchester Garrison as a member of the Voluntary Aid Detachment. She died in 1973 in Sevenoaks, aged 81. Sybil moved to India after World War II and married Graham Ogilvy, who had been a regular officer in the Indian Army from World War I. They married in 1923 in Quetta. They subsequently moved to South Africa where Sybil died in 1976.

Additionally, Yvonne Watts put us in touch with her sister-in-law Eileen Harrington (nee Watts) who was at CCHS in the 1940s. Eileen told us of her mother Beryl (born 1900) who went to school at Grey Friars when she was 5, as one of the first pupils enrolled after the nuns founded their convent and school.

Any further information about people connected with Grey Friars during this period would be much appreciated as it would greatly enhance the social history of the site. The project is on-going, care of the website: www.greyfriarscolchester.org.uk

Colchester County High School for Girls   The CCHS minute book tells that Grey Friars was purchased circa 1920 in order to house the Lower School and free-up space in the North Hill building (now Colchester Sixth Form College). "The staff room was taken over for a form room, there were classes in the corridor, coachings in every corner and even the gallery was used, a wooden trellis being erected to prevent those from above who were more interested in gym than geometry joining the class below head first! Great was the relief when the Essex Education Committee took over Grey Friars and it was decided to house the Junior School there, together with Miss Harris and the Preparatory which had hitherto been functioning in St Peter's rooms."

Unfortunately, there was a scare in the first term when the roof was discovered to be on fire; the first call on the newly-installed telephone was to the fire brigade. The minute book records: "Imagine our dismay when the hose burst in the top corridor and water poured through the ceilings, down the stairs in a torrent and out the front door. It meant a day's holiday for us and might have meant much more. Face to face with impending disaster we realised as never before what a precious possession Grey Friars was to us."

(above) CCHS Lower School 1923   (below) details showing (left) preparatory pupils including boys and (right) the staff

A note was sent to Joan Gurney in 1999 (in response to a previous publication about CCHS) from a former pupil at Colchester Royal Grammar School, Hardy Frost, who had previously been one of the small boys in the Preparatory Department of CCHS in the days when young boys were also admitted (see detail below).

The CCHS tenure lasted for 37 years, when the school moved en bloc to new accommodation in Norman Way, where it remains to this day. Grey Friars is remembered with reverence and affection by many who attended during that time. "Coming from a small village as a scholarship entrant I was completely

overawed by Grey Friars," says Mrs Page. "The main staircase was like one in a country house, and we had to change into 'house shoes' when we arrived. The grounds at the back were spacious and beautiful. There was a lawn dominated by a very large, spreading holm oak tree, and on a lower level another lawn with the remains of a conservatory. We weren't allowed in there as it was unsafe. It was covered in wisteria, beautiful when in bloom. Before I finish I must mention a 'secret' passage which went from the upper floors, down a winding staircase, and came out of the panelling near the dining room. It was the thing to do it once and appear suddenly in front of those coming out of the dining room. Of course we weren't supposed to use it!"

The late Margaret Sherry Podgorska, CCHS 1930s, writes "I started school at Grey Friars in the Lower 2nd in the autumn of 1930. Looking back more than half a century later, I realised just how much my school days at Grey Friars shaped the pattern of my whole life as a writer, globetrotter and passionate student of history." In later life, Margaret became a staunch supporter of Grey Friars as an adult college and all it stood for in the community.

Temporary residents   Monkwick School (later re-named Thomas, Lord Audley School) was formed in 1958, when classes from Wilson Marriage School moved temporarily to Grey Friars. Philip Morant School was established in 1963, similarly starting at Grey Friars and moving on in 1965.

The beginning of Monkwick School – housed temporarily in Grey Friars in 1958 (photo courtesy Ron Harvey)

The Technical College (now Colchester Institute) also used the premises temporarily. As a music student in the 1960s Sheila Scott remembers when the building housed the music school of the rapidly-growing college. Her husband Don remembers impressive photographs in a local newspaper when pianos were manoeuvred by crane when they decamped to new premises in Sheepen Road. Formerly a CCHS pupil at Grey Friars, Sheila was also a student during its time as an adult college, and then acted as pianist, latterly tutor, for choral classes. Local historian Andrew Phillips, a senior member of the Institute staff until retirement, remembers their Grey Friars tenancy well. He, in common with many, remarks at Grey Friars' disproportionately large impact on people, considering their relatively short periods of occupation. As well as large, noisy instruments blasting forth in the elegant Georgian spaces, he remembers the Drama Department's conversion of the former chapel into a studio, run by "the enthusiastic and undefeatable Nesta Slack", completing a picture of artistic vibrancy within the buildings – soon to be replicated when the Adult Community College curriculum developed in the 1990s.

Adult Education Originally, adult education also had the status of a temporary resident, existing alongside other occupants in the partially-vacant buildings. It had been identified that spare capacity at Grey Friars presented the ideal opportunity to host daytime classes for adults, as well as providing an administrative base separately identifiable from the schools being used for evening classes. When the other users eventually moved on to their brand-new buildings, adult education was left as the only occupant and it was feared that the premises might be declared redundant, vacated and sold. But with the need for daytime classes increasing, and the overall programme (day, evening and weekend) rapidly expanding, space was urgently required not only to accommodate the courses, but also to provide essential support services such as a crèche, enquiries facilities, offices, catering and common rooms.

Securing the venue, however, was less a matter of strategy on the part of the responsible authority and more a mixture of foresight, good judgement and opportunism in 1965 on the part of Allin Coleman. A local teacher who became the first Grey Friars principal, he was trusted and supported by local education officers. Previously, adult education classes were managed from Alderman Blaxill School and held during the evenings in venues throughout the town. Now, with its own premises, a high-profile building of substance and repute, known by generations of Colchester people, and in a central location, the scene was set for the development of an education institution especially for adults. So from the 'Senior Evening Institute' of the 1960s came the seeds of what was to grow into 'The Adult Community College' of the 1990s … and securing Grey Friars as the main base was the turning point.

In her foreword to a book about the work of the adult college, Baroness Helena Kennedy QC wrote: "Grey Friars is a special place. It should be on the Grand Tour of every new education minister before wheels are reinvented and new-fangled schemes are cobbled together to deal with skills shortages and social exclusion, anti-social behaviour and civic regeneration." Having chaired the Government's 'Learning Works' report on the benefits of adult learning, her extensive evidence-gathering gave her a real insight into the social and economic contribution made by adult colleges.

In the years following Kennedy's 1997 report, there was much debate in education circles about the content, style and mode of delivery of learning in later life. The ethos developed from its first years with the provision of support services (common rooms, catering, crèche, study area, library, tutorials, advice and guidance sessions) and community involvement (governors, Members' Association, a travelling classroom to take the experience throughout the area) meant Colchester ticked all the boxes. Underpinning all of this was the flagship, Grey Friars, within which the careful nurturing of a welcoming, relaxed yet business-like environment set the tone for local adult community learning for decades.

Local people testified to the value of such an environment. "Setting foot in the main entrance I saw the glass case exhibiting the latest achievements of students, and the walls festooned with even more notices suggesting, exhorting, encouraging. People smiled in greeting, although many were strangers. The whole place called out, 'Come on! What are you waiting for?' " explained Valerie Elliston. Dorothy Schwarz, a local author and enthusiastic tutor, called it "The Grey Friars Effect. That almost indescribable something that affects students, tutors and others who work here." A belief shared by all three principals was that having a venue such as Grey Friars within which to develop the curriculum and support services was crucial for any adult college to fulfil its community-orientated role.

Allin Coleman (1965-73)   Enid Bishop (1973-83)   Alan Skinner (1983-2005)
40 years of Grey Friars principals, 1965 to 2005

Ofsted witnessed this in their 1995 inspection and, although they described it in their own (highly quantitative) terms, still managed to capture that special feel: "Students participate fully in the classes and learn with enthusiasm; they support each other and benefit from well organised and carefully planned sessions. The quality of learning was satisfactory in 21% of classes, good in 66% and very good in 13%. 97% teaching is satisfactory or better; 76% was good or very good. Staff support students in a positive manner and encourage them to extend themselves. Students are confident, serious learners and make good progress. In some areas of the curriculum, such as art and craft, students achieve high standards and produce excellent work. The college has a committed and loyal student body." It was widely acknowledged that the ambience of Grey Friars as a location contributed greatly to its effectiveness.

Showing how much they value their adult college – a group prepares to lobby parliament to prevent drastic changes being made.

Claire Hawkins, who taught English and was a tutor on the scheme giving adults access to university education, once commented that "Grey Friars is actually a humane place," alluding to its person-centred ethos, but also, along with many others, contrasting its setting to the more common perception of an educational institution – what adult student Roger Moores called "today's grey, glass-walled exam-factories." Roger, a retired industrial relations advisor came first to computer classes and then progressed to more creative studies. "Experts may say that Grey Friars is not fit for purpose … it is old, rambling, squeaky … needs a lift … it is just a comfortable, friendly old town house … You are welcome, there's an atmosphere." Many maintain that the Grey Friars environment encouraged and contributed to positive learning experiences which changed people's lives for the better.

Tutor Maggie Bernstein said, "Colleagues work hard to retain the familial atmosphere without compromising their professional attitudes to the learning process." In fact, teachers often reached the highest professional standards, as evidenced by awards for high achievement won from examining authorities. Grey Friars students often ranked with the best schools and colleges nationally and in fact, until the reorganisation of examining bodies, the college's achievements were, literally, second to none.

The Grey Friars name became national news when yet another press release from the Associated Examining Board declared the college "Top of the league for top-performing A-Level students for the fourth time since the awards began in 1986" The list of high achievers who studied (part-time it should be remembered) at Grey Friars is impressive. Subjects in which they excelled included French, Business Studies, English Literature, Economic & Social History, Sociology and Fashion Design. In sport, Grey Friars also excelled. Without a swimming pool of its own, it became a nationally recognised centre for swimming teaching and the training of teachers, and also won awards for the very high number of adults who learnt to swim, including those with disabilities.

The Grey Friars summer schools (tutored by leading academics, artists and craftspeople) attracted enrolments from far and wide. A profile of the college in a national adult education journal included a snippet of college life and a photograph of a middle-aged woman and her bicycle in front of Grey Friars. She looked as if she had just pedalled from the other side of town. Not so! She turned out to be a student who had earlier surprised staff with a telephone call from Rotterdam to check if all was well with the three-day patchwork course. Meike van Floudt was about to set off on her bicycle to catch the ferry to Harwich.

On another occasion, a fax arrived from Japan asking for an urgent faxback of the prospectus – followed soon after by a request for some course description sheets for a professor from Keio University, Tokyo, who was coming to England. A fax and credit card enrolment from Mrs van der Watt from Reitz, South Africa caused a stir in the office when she contacted Grey Friars to enrol for some art courses run by Royal Academicians. And notable addresses appearing in the mailing list for 2003/4 included Alicante, Denmark and two from Scotland – rendering others such as Oxfordshire and Berkshire comparatively local!

There is no doubt that the ambience which pervaded the environment within the walls of the complex assisted greatly in this and, despite housing an institution rather than a family, the buildings aided the task. Even the school extensions suited this purpose, their design and atmosphere borrowing heavily from the core building, the family house. This aspect has been particularly valuable in providing a suitable setting for the college's work with more vulnerable groups within society such as adults with learning difficulties, school-refusing teenagers, those for whom English is not the first language and people in rehabilitation from medical or other traumas.

Grey Friars as an adult college also had an influence beyond its walls. One of the college's firm commitments was to work outside the 'normal' educational environment. As well as standard classes located in schools and halls around the borough it was felt that non-traditional settings should be utilised. To this end, a 'travelling classroom' was built on a lorry chassis and taken to venues such as supermarkets and industrial premises, often in partnership with other organisations, but always using the 'Grey Friars' brand.

The travelling classroom at a local Co-Operative supermarket to give 'taster' classes   An IT introductory session in progress

A maisonette on the Greenstead estate hired by the college as the focus of a community learning project in the 1990s was known as "the Grey Friars flat". Many people used to say "I go to a Grey Friars class in Stanway School, (or Tiptree, or Wivenhoe)". Although not all of the work and achievement of this community-based college took place in Grey Friars, as the centre of operations it was the flagship – a symbol and a brand-name. For many thousands of Colchester people, over a period exceeding 30 years, for 'adult education' you would read 'Grey Friars'.

A perfect example of this comes from 1986, when, following one of the many proposed reorganisations of Essex community education, County Hall officials were considering combining adult education, youth services and youth vocational training in Colchester. A vigorous community and media campaign was fought to prevent Grey Friars being closed and sold. "Grey

Friars needs to be at Grey Friars" wrote Fiona Rudd to the County Standard. The idea was eventually dropped and Brooklands youth house and the former East Ward school were sold instead, with their services transferred to the redundant Wilson Marriage School.

Staff, governors and volunteers of the Adult Community College in 1996

However, nearly twenty years later, in 2005, during yet another period of 're-shaping' of its services, Essex County Council once again proposed disposal of premises and reorganisation of adult education. This time it was accompanied by a major realignment of management, with the withdrawal of local influence (no Principal and educational management team in Colchester, no Colchester governors) and Grey Friars lost its college status. Again, there was vociferous objection locally, but with all managerial decisions made from County Hall in Chelmsford, Grey Friars was eventually listed for disposal, the curriculum was reduced and remaining classes moved to the Wilson Marriage building, away from the town centre. This venue, ironically, had been saved by amalgamation with Grey Friars in an earlier partial reorganisation by the County Council. After protracted retrenchment and decline, the 'for sale' signs went up on Grey Friars' façade in 2007 and the educational era ended after 103 years of hosting learning for local people, young and old.

Continuing the Lifelong Learning Tradition   In a remarkable twist of fate, despite no longer being a place of learning, Grey Friars still encourages and enthuses local people in the quest for knowledge and understanding.

There was an overwhelming response from local people and tourists during the 2007 Heritage Open Weekend exhibition and tours organised to mark the closure of the adult college after 40 years at Grey Friars. This book followed; interest in the preparation of the book resulted in invitations to lecture on its findings; lectures prompted responses from the community – and turned the whole enterprise into an on-going community education project.

Contributions began coming in from across the world via the project's website www.greyfriarscolchester.org which continues the research into the site's historical, social, archaeological and architectural significance (in effect, constantly updating this book) by encouraging participation from all with Grey Friars connections or interest.

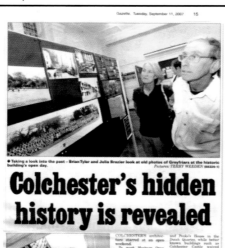

The exhibition on the history of the site attracted much interest (left) as did conducted tours of the building (right).
ECN

7
C21st • Now and the future

Renaissance At the time of writing, after a considerable time lying vacant and on the market, Grey Friars and Hillcrest, along with All Saints House next door, have been acquired by a company with a high-quality portfolio of High Street retail, business and hotel properties.

Conversion to a luxury hotel using all three buildings is in progress. It is encouraging to witness the standard of care taken in the renovations and the sympathetic nature of the additions joining the premises to form a new entrance (photos OMCI).

Archaeological finds   The site of the Grey Friars' settlement has been subject to major disturbance over the last couple of hundred years, but relatively little has been discovered about the friary itself. The Colchester Archaeological Trust (CAT) has taken a great deal of interest in the site and gives us the best analysis of what is known so far. It is noted, however, that compared to the documentary evidence, the archaeological evidence is sparse.

Some of the earliest recorded attempts to interpret the site through archaeology come from the mid-1800s, when the Botanic Gardens failed and began to be redeveloped. In one of her extensive reports for the Trust, Kate Orr tells us that William Wire (the diarist quoted previously with reference to balloon flights above the site) recorded between 1847 and 1857 the discovery of several skeletons at Grey Friars. On the lot map accompanying the 1847 sale catalogue for Grey Friars, Wire (see Appendix) wrote that they were found in the kitchen garden and that he believed they were probably inmates from the friary. The upper car-park (behind All Saints House) is on the site of the kitchen garden. Wire wrote (usefully, albeit not entirely accurately):

"The whole of this property belonged to a monastic order named the Grey or preaching friars for an account of see Morants History of Colchester and Fosbroke's Monachesm all attempts to get at the desired information as to whereabouts the monastery stood has failed unless it occupied the site of the dwelling house forming part of lot 1 [The current Grey Friars centre section of 1755/80] as that is still known by the name of The Friery no foundations that I am aware of have been discovered in the Botanic Garden and the only remains of a building was a stone window discovered a few years ago and which I believe is now ornamenting the garden in detached pieces instead of whitened flint stones. In the garden of lot 1 several Roman coins have been found and in the kitchen garden at the depth of about four feet from the surface skeletons have been discovered ranging from east to west the head towards the former point the feet of one being placed against the head of the other not a fragment of wearing apparel was discovered with them nor yet any ornaments the skulls had low foreheads and the teeth worn down by grinding giving the same idea of the monks general character who occupied the premises as that related of them by writers on the monastic orders."

During works to convert Grey Friars and Hillcrest to a convent school in 1904 some coins were found: a second brass of Vespasian; a plated denarius of Saloninus, a bronze Constantinian and a very small late bronze coin.

To the north of the car-park, a watching brief on ground-works at the rear of 67 Castle Road in 1997 recorded a late medieval pit or trench containing food waste and domestic rubbish which is probably associated with the friary. To the west, a long archaeological trench excavated by the Colchester Excavation Committee at the front of the former Central Clinic in 1963 recorded early medieval pottery at the east end, giving a hint of the proximity of the friary.

In recent years, CAT has carried out various small digs at Grey Friars on the occasion of minor ground-works or building adjustments to the site. These and previous investigations had tantalisingly demonstrated the existence of medieval, post-medieval and possibly Roman archaeological features, most of which are to be found at approximately 1m below ground-level. Some Romano-British material was also found. There have been possible Roman features, robbed-out foundations, but they could equally have been medieval as much Roman material was recycled in later buildings. Roman artefacts were found mixed in with deposits from later periods in several places throughout the site. One Roman coin, several tesserae, some opus signinum mortar (containing crushed Roman tile), and a small quantity of Roman pottery were retrieved from trenches in the north-east corner of the car park. Particularly evident in abundance was Roman tile, most likely having been reused in the medieval buildings.

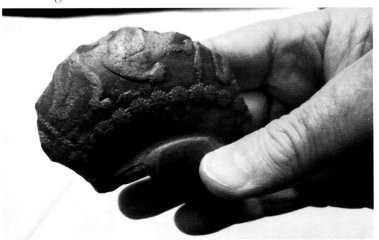

From Castle Road – base and side of Samian Ware Roman drinking vessel (CAT)

In the 1990s, pieces of Samian pottery were spotted when a flowerbed was being dug over in Grey Friars, the material having been transferred in soil which had come from a house in Roman Road. These were similar to fragments and rim sherds found on land at 41 Castle Road in 2000, which also included some hypocaust tile fragments. Work at 24 Castle Road in 2000/1 revealed small quantities of Roman pottery, mortar, tile and tesserae (cubes of stone used for flooring and mosaics).

Tile from Castle Road (LM)

Samian Ware fragment from Roman Road (CAT)

A tessellated floor (made of tesserae, laid on a bed of mortar) was recorded to the rear of the Grey Friars building in 2004, at 1.1m below ground-level. This appeared to be part of a house that faced the main Roman road later to become Frere (Friar) Street and High Street, but very little else was found.

Whereabouts the floor was located within the house would be an important fact to establish, as a precise location of the line of the Roman street would assist in the interpretation of some of the earlier maps which seem to suggest that the building line prior to the Georgian period may have been further back from the present pavement. This, together with closer investigation of the structures in the cellars of the current buildings - if proved - may explain the appearance of the convoluted southern boundary to the site shown in the C17th maps.

Further south, towards the High Street, no foundations were exposed but there were two probable medieval sand-quarry pits. A linear spread of building rubble appeared to have functioned as some kind of surface or walkway. This and a large pit filled with building rubble were most likely derived from demolished friary buildings such as the church, cloister, precinct wall or gatehouse. Although no graves were exposed, one piece of skull was found near the north edge of the upper car park (behind All Saints House, near the location of skeletons found in the 1800s), but had probably already been moved from its original position. Activity following the Dissolution was evidenced by a number of spreads of building rubble. In 2007, a wide medieval foundation which may represent part of the friary church was found on the unpaved area between the upper and lower car parks. Its size, east-west alignment and medieval pottery associated with it all support this theory.

Part of the supposed foundation of the church of the Grey Friars, exposed in early 2007 © CAT

Next to it was a large amount of building rubble. A copper-alloy buckle 'typical of that worn on a monk's girdle' was found amongst this rubble. Three pieces of floor tile and four fragments of worked stone all suggested a friary building. A further medieval wall foundation, at right-angles to another and probably part of the same building or perhaps a cloister attached to the church was found in the north-east area of the car park. The layer of demolition debris sealing these features contained medieval and post-medieval material indicating that these buildings continued in use well after the Dissolution of 1538 as evidenced by records of the redistribution of ownership by the King's agents (see Chronology which follows). This also ties-in with the various early maps and drawings showing friary buildings set back some distance from the main street, with a large gap between them and the gatehouse. How far north the buildings reached, however, is still a mystery. Exploratory trenches dug when the northern car park wall was being rebuilt were inconclusive, rarely reaching natural ground. The friars' calling, however, suggests that their church would be the building nearest to the public highway (for accessibility), with their domestic buildings further back.

A WW2 air-raid shelter was also exposed, dating to the time of the site's use as the County High School for Girls. This had unfortunately been cut into the area which revealed possible church foundations. Several other post-medieval pits and ditches were exposed. The medieval and post-medieval pottery from the site was identified to be of higher status than that of a normal domestic site. The date of the pottery relates to the very end of the friary's existence as a religious establishment, and quite possibly to the time of the Dissolution and the early years of its use as a secular site. The amount and distribution of building rubble found during the Trust's investigations substantiates the evidence from maps and drawings illustrated earlier in this section that the buildings were not completely demolished until the 18th century.

More recently, in March 2013, a draining trench in the yard between Grey Friars and All Saints House revealed evidence of a Roman mortar floor and part of a (possibly later) foundation. The floor may have been associated with a Roman house facing the High Street, far enough away from the 2004 find to be a separate house. Broken pottery, tile and brick were found in the spoil from the digging. The scarcity of substantial Roman features may be explained by later disturbance or masking by medieval and post-medieval activities. One piece of Anglo-Saxon pottery, found in the north-east corner of the car park, hinted at occupation on the site between the 5th and the 7th centuries, but as it was likely to have been moved from its original position it was not significant proof.

Line of mortar floor in a Roman house discovered at Grey Friars. (CAT)

C19/20th bottles found in a rubbish pit during a dig on the Grey Friars site February 2013 (CAT).
The centre bottle is marked E.T.PROSSER and is from the chemist's shop at 7 Head Street 1866 – 1899.

The most notable of recent finds, however, pre-dates even the Roman period. During works to prepare for the new hotel, a flint weapon was discovered. As flint cannot be carbon-dated, museum experts were consulted and they concluded that the object was an early Bronze Age dagger of between 2500BC and 1750BC. The type of material and the way it was formed suggest that it was an import from north Germany. Regarded as a very important find, a spokesperson for the museum service said that it was 'of major significance' because flint daggers of this kind, thought to be ceremonial items of high status, are rare in Essex. It was found by a worker digging foundations. Don Shimmin, one of the CAT archaeologists keeping a watch on activities at the site said, "Its discovery was a complete fluke. There's nothing like it been found in Colchester before."

Views of the flint dagger (courtesy CAT ©)

These painstaking evaluations by the Trust, often under time pressure and in constricted space, have clearly demonstrated the survival of Roman, medieval and post-medieval archaeological features on the site, most of which are to be found at approximately 1m below ground-level. Unfortunately, without larger-scale and deeper excavations, allowing what is discovered to be viewed in a wider context, we have to be content with small snapshots of the archaeology leading to best-guess interpretations of what was once there.

 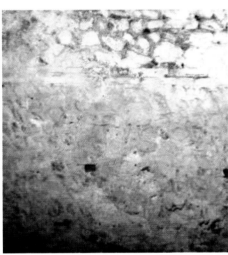

Re-used materials are in abundance across the site.
Above: Intriguing material in the cellar walls of All Saints House (LPP)

Grey Friars Site Chronology

Relevant national events			Grey Friars site developments
43	Roman invasion	circa 44	Temple of Claudius built on site now occupied by the castle. Fort and a later civilian settlement built where the modern town centre now stands.
		circa 60/61	Boudicca's forces destroyed the settlement.
		circa 70	Town rebuilt with substantial ramparts and walls. The first enclosure of the site destined to become Grey Friars.
409	Roman rule ends	410	Viking and Anglo-Saxon period begins. No significant evidence.
1066-1087	Norman invasion William I	circa 1069	Colchester's castle built over podium of the Temple of Claudius. Much adjacent land came under royal control.
1216	Henry III	1224	Franciscans arrived in England. Grey Friars later occupied land along High St between castle and eastern walls.
		1237	King granted the Grey Friars some land to enlarge their site within Colchester's walls
		1247	King gave the friars 10 marks, possibly for further building.
		1269	King gave the friars 7 oaks to build their church.
1272	Edward I	1279	Friars permitted to bring water by conduit across King's land under town wall.
		1306	King gave the friars 6 oaks, possibly for further building.
1307	Edward II	1300s and 1400s	Further donations of land and materials from royalty, nobility, gentry and others. The Franciscan friary eventually filled at least the north-east corner of the town's walls.
1509	Henry VIII	1536	Dissolution of monasteries, whole Grey Friars site surrendered to King's agent by 1538.
		1544	Francis Jobson had the site granted to him by the Crown.
1547 1553 1558-1603	Edward VI Mary I Elizabeth I	1565	Jobson conveyed site to William Watson. Brian and John Watson later received the site in bequest.
		1586	Brian Watson conveyed his share to Martin Basil.
		1596	William Watson conveyed his share to Martin Basil who later passed site to son and grandson.
1625-49	Charles I	1636	Site conveyed to Henry Leming and son Henry.
1642-1651	Civil War	1648	'Fryar's Yard' used to house Royalist soldiers taken captive by Sir Thomas Fairfax whose army had held Colchester under siege
1649-59	Republic	1654	Lemings sold site to William Peeke.
1694 1702 1714	William III Anne George I	1700	Thomas Turgis (who married Peeke's daughter) conveyed site to Thomas Carpenter. Carpenter bequeathed site to his grandson Thomas Bayes.
1727	George II	1740	Bayes sold site to Robert Potter.
		1752	Potter died; site sold to Rev. John Halls around that time
		1755	Halls built the present house and laid out new gardens.
1760	George III	1780	'Garden front' built to the rear of the house.
		1795	Halls' nephew James inherits Grey Friars and leases out.
		c1814	Halls' nephew James sold to Thomas Baskerfield
		1817	Property willed to Baskerfield's wife Sophia with his executor Horatio Cock and heirs.

1820	George IV	1824	Priory Field (behind the house's formal gardens) leased to trustees of the Colchester and Essex Botanical and Horticultural Society.
1837	Victoria	1841	Grey Friars possibly occupied by tenants, the Bawtree family: Charles aged 35 a Merchant, his wife Eliza and 4 children and 3 servants.
		1848	Rev John Robert Smythies in residence.
		1849	Stephen Brown bought house from heirs of Horatio Cock.
		1851	Botanic Gardens failed and offered for sale in lots. Roman and Castle roads laid out.
		1853	By this time, Brown had secured extra land to form the present rectangular site.
		1871	Grey Friars possibly occupied by tenant Sayers Turner an attorney, his wife Louisa and 5 children and 4 servants.
		1874	Post Office directory showed Captain Fitzroy Wilson in residence.
		1881	Census showed Major John Radcliffe in residence
		1891	Owner Rev Canon J.H. Marsden died. Census showed Lieutenant Colonel William Marsden and family in residence
		1891	Trustees of Rev Canon J.H. Marsden sold to Dr E.L. Fenn
1901	Edward VII	1903	Dr Fenn sold the house and gardens to the Sisters (or Ladies) of Nazareth, likely to be of the Franciscan order.
1910	George V	1904	New extensions for convent and school joined up Grey Friars with Hillcrest
1914-1918	World War One	1919	Convent, school and grounds sold to Essex County Council.
		1920	Colchester County High School for Girls moved into Grey Friars. The Preparatory department moved in from St Peter's Rooms and the Junior department from North Hill (a site shared with the Technical Institute).
1936	Edward VIII		
1936	George VI		
1939-45	World War Two		
1952	Elizabeth II	1957	Colchester County High School for Girls moved to new premises in Norman Way, Lexden Road.
		1958	Some Wilson Marriage School classes arrived at Grey Friars to form the beginning of Monkwick School, before moving on to purpose-built premises.
		1963	Philip Morant School founded at Grey Friars before moving to purpose-built premises.
			The Music School of the N.E.Essex Technical College temporarily resident during the 1960s.
		1965	Colchester's Senior Evening Institute took residence for offices and daytime classes, later developing into the Adult Community College for the area.
		2005	Essex County Council reviewed their adult education provision county-wide and withdrew all local management, governance and college status from Grey Friars.
		2007	Premises vacated and offered for sale.
		2014	Conversion to a hotel complex completed.

Part Two

•

Architecture

•

The Georgian family home

(JG)

Introduction

In the early C17th there was a revolution in British architecture when the neo-classical style finally came to England. It was based on that of Greece and Rome (first to fourth century) and influenced by the Renaissance in Italy (fifteenth to sixteenth century). During the next two hundred years it would transform the way the British built their houses. Inigo Jones (1573-1652) brought classical architecture to Britain. Twice in the early C17th he visited Italy and studied monuments of ancient Rome. He used as his guide "The Four Books of Architecture" by the Italian architect Palladio (1508-1580). One of Inigo Jones's early commissions was to design the Queen's House in Greenwich, and later the Banqueting House in Whitehall.

The story of Grey Friars as it stands today begins in 1755 when the Rev John Halls, vicar of Easthorpe, wanted a town house, and he "built a very handsome house" better described as a small mansion for himself and his wife Elizabeth Selley, when they married in 1747. He also shared the house with his mother-in-law. The details of the house taken from Morant's second edition of his "History and Antiqueties of Colchester" 1768 state that the Rev John Halls "made good gardens with other improvements." One of the main functions of the house was therefore to impress.

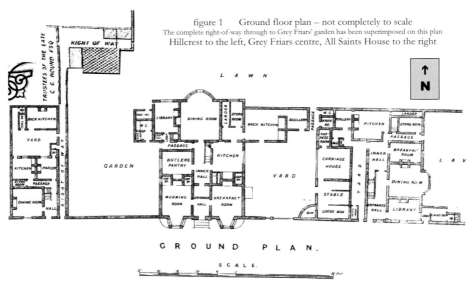

figure 1   Ground floor plan – not completely to scale
The complete right-of-way through to Grey Friars' garden has been superimposed on this plan
Hillcrest to the left, Grey Friars centre, All Saints House to the right

This plan represents the range of buildings at the end of the 19th century.

Evidence of skilled craftsmanship can still be seen throughout the building with a great deal of elaborate plaster and woodwork in some rooms. The simpler nature of two of them may suggest that they were for Halls' own use (perhaps a concession to his calling), leaving the more opulent areas for his wife's use. He added the north-facing "Garden Front" in 1780.

In 1904 a group of French nuns (The Sisters of Nazareth) added the east and west wings after being driven away from France by the restrictions of the Law of Associations. They are thought to have settled first at the Minories – just over the road – and then when the extensions to Grey Friars were completed, they moved in. They may have required large rooms for use as workshops because they were embroiderers. They also included a chapel in which to celebrate their faith. Their newly acquired space also allowed them to open a school in 1910. They may have lived in the small late C18th building of Hillcrest, next door on the western side, using Grey Friars as their workplace.

It is known from plans of the period (figure 1) that there was a pre-existing right-of-way through Hillcrest to Grey Friars, and during the alterations made by the Sisters of Nazareth in 1904 the right-of-way was extended, further covered over and became an integral part of the combined buildings (fig 2).

East Hill, Colchester.

The "IXL" Series.

fig 2   Postcard from before 1904
Next to the man walking on the pavement, the smaller door marks the right-of-way entry point for the passage passing through Hillcrest, and leading across the back to the Grey Friars garden.

91

The present building of Grey Friars therefore has three distinct stages – 1755, 1780 and 1904, but the sum of the parts has retained the neo-classical style. Neo-classical buildings were always very symmetrical and built with special emphasis on the outside and its appearance – rather than from the functions of the various rooms inside. The Palladian influence ensured that, externally, a mirror image was invariably achieved and whatever architectural features appeared on the left also appeared on the right (fig 3). Plans of neo-classical buildings were also drawn up to encourage the standardisation of design.

fig 3 (OMCI)

HILLCREST   WEST WING   GREY FRIARS   EAST WING

No further large structural alterations were made to the building from 1920 to 1957 when it was occupied by the Preparatory and Junior Departments of Colchester County High School for Girls, and the grounds and gardens were maintained as elegantly as before, although the imposing conservatory was by now beginning to fall into disrepair.

The building was listed Grade II* in 1950 and its educational function continued from 1957 to 2008 when it was the headquarters of Colchester's Adult Community College. Its delightful garden, however, gradually disappeared to give way to car-parking facilities as the quest and need for learning and qualifications in adult life increased.

The following section of the book looks at the architecture of the existing building and relates that to its occupants – the householders, nuns, schoolchildren and adult students who have passed through its doors. Evidence of previous buildings and archaeological remains are also explored and after this initial overview the text is written in the form of a guided tour which looks at the exterior, interior and grounds through the eyes of numerous generations of occupants, and the traces of seven distinct phases through which the site has passed.

1
Setting in context

Grey Friars is very much part of a group of neo-classical buildings which stretch along this part of the High Street and down both sides of East Hill, many of them sharing the distinctive features which define neo-classicism. However, within this little oasis there is much evidence of earlier occupancies. Grey Friars stands on the same side of the road as the Norman castle to the west (fig 4) and all around there are reminders of Roman times. There are also Victorian flourishes, Gothic-style extravagancies, modern C21st architecture and many of these reveal Colchester's role in art and education. All these are worth exploring by visitors to Colchester.

fig4   fig 5

On the opposite side of the road, a little to the west of Grey Friars, is the Minories (number 74 High Street). This house (fig 5) in a very similar style to Grey Friars, was bought in 1731 by Isaac Boggis a merchant in the wool trade. The house remained in the family for nearly 200 years. In 1776 Thomas Boggis, who was an alderman and mayor of the town, bought number 73 which partially overlapped number 74, and refurbished the latter in the same Palladian style as Grey Friars.

Similarities between the two are still evident. In 1923 Geoffrey Bensusan-Butt bought the houses number 73 and 74 together with the land to the south of the garden which contained a Gothic-style folly known firstly as the Dovecot and later as the Summer House. In 1958 number 74 was opened as an art gallery and extended into number 73 in 1976. Currently, they form part of Colchester Institute's facilities for post-graduate study in art and the ground floor remains an art gallery.

fig 6

fig 7

Immediately opposite Grey Friars is another neo-classical building – East Hill House (fig 6). It was rebuilt by George Wegg in about 1730. The extensive gardens ran from the Roman wall adjoining Priory Street and the churchyard of St James' passing behind the houses on that side of the road, almost to Queen Street. At the western end of this long garden the Gothic-style folly was created around 1745 inspired by some of the standardised plans made available for restored ancient architecture (fig 7). It was intended as a fanciful garden shelter and this folly now stands in the present garden of the Minories. It is, of course, a very early eccentric example of the Gothic revival period (now listed grade II) and dating even before Strawberry Hill was designed and built by Horace Walpole. East Hill House itself has an imposing frontage to the High Street and an early photographic postcard of the rear (fig 8) written

East Hill House

fig 8

in 1904 seems to confirm that it once had a function as a Dame School. As well as the message on the back that "the children have cameras of their own and have taken the photograph" the writer indicates on the front that "all the top rooms are the schoolroom apartments which I have to keep tidy. You won't see all the school room windows as they (*the children*) have not got this all in – you can only see one." The atmosphere of this type of school with its individual approach, strict discipline and ethic of respect can be captured by viewing Frederick George Cotman's painting "The Dame School" 1887 held by Colchester and Ipswich Museum Services (fig 8b).

fig 8b   CIMS

One of the most pleasurable aspects in the rear garden at East Hill House is the giant spreading mulberry tree (fig 9). Tymperleys, the former clock museum, also has a mulberry tree, as once did Grey Friars. Schoolchildren from nearby schools, including Colchester County High School, reared their silkworms on mulberry leaves and creatively spun silk from their cocoons (see Appendix).

Close by the north frontage of East Hill House, at pavement level, is a Victorian drinking fountain inscribed with the words "With joy shall ye draw water. Erected by MR 1864." (fig 10) Between the Minories and East Hill

House and set back from the High Street on land which originally joined the two together is Colchester's most modern piece of architecture, Firstsite.

fig 9

Designed by Raphael Vinoly, the gilded alloy crescent-shaped arts centre opened in September 2011 amidst great controversy over its cost. (fig 11)

fig 10

fig 11

Only a short distance from Grey Friars' front door and part-way down East Hill is the Roman wall which originally completely encircled the town. A plaque high up on a house indicates that this is also the former position of East Gate which fell down in 1651 (figs 12 and 13). Another plaque, recently unveiled at number 8 East Hill, commemorates the artist Frank Daniell, 1866-1932. An East Gate interpretation board is planned by the Civic Society.

From here it is possible to follow the wall as it progresses northwards and then turns westwards towards Duncan's Gate. This is beyond Roman Road, behind the present Grey Friars building, marking the northern boundary of what was formerly land occupied by the Franciscan Friars. Duncan's Gate (fig 14) was one of six gates through which movement took place in Roman Colchester. The remains of only two of the six gates survive above ground, the most visible and complete of which is Balkerne Gate on the western side of town. Other openings in the wall were made during the medieval period.

fig 12

fig 13

Duncan's Gate, the nearest to Grey Friars, was built about AD65 to 80 and was named after the doctor who excavated it in 1853. The town's defences were strengthened in the C4th and the gate went out of use and was blocked.

fig 14

The gatehouse originally had an upper storey which collapsed hundreds of years ago, but from the inside of today's ruin the remains of an arched window can be seen. From Duncan's Gate the Roman wall continues westward and as it passes to the north of Colchester Castle it completes the little quadrant in the north-east corner of Colchester which encloses Grey Friars and forms the focal point of this book.

2
The frontage

Grey Friars, as it now stands, presents an array of fine and elaborate external and internal classical features which largely go unnoticed, and whose importance is generally unrecognised. Many of these features equal those in better known neo-classical buildings scattered throughout the country.

Classical architecture, such as that of Grey Friars was originally developed in ancient Greece (from 400BC) and it was then adapted and extended by the Romans (C1st to C4th), rediscovered and modified during the Renaissance (C15th to C17th) finally being brought to Great Britain in the C17th and known thereafter as neo-classicism. The Greek influence brought verticals and horizontals; the Roman influence arches and domes. The Romans relied heavily on the writings of the architect Vitruvius for their definitions. Classical architecture was influenced by mathematical principles and was based on 'Orders' which were a kind of architectural code or grammar relating to shape, proportion and decoration, and which had to be followed carefully in all constructions. Each Order had its own mathematical rules. The core of this code was the vertical supporting column and its supported lintel. The column consisted of a base, shaft and capital (its summit) and the lintel (or entablature) consisted of the architrave, frieze and cornice.

Of the five Orders three are considered to derive from the purer Greek forms (Doric, Ionic and Corinthian) and two are Roman additions (Tuscan and Composite). They are arranged in a hierarchy (fig 15) and have recognisable features. This hierarchy, from the simple to the more elaborate, can often be seen starting on the lower floors of a building and moving upwards; externally and internally, and it is sometimes used as a social label for the occupants.

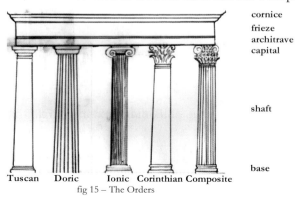

fig 15 – The Orders

The Tuscan Order is the most primitive of them all with a plain, smooth column and a simple capital. The Doric Order has more 'masculine' columns associated with strength and which have sharp-edged grooves; there is often no base. The capital is plain, convex and cushion shaped. The Ionic Order is much taller, more elegant, slender and 'feminine'. The shaft is often grooved (fluted) but with very flat bands. The most recognisable feature is the capital which has two in-curled scrolls or volutes. The Corinthian Order is also very 'feminine' and is characterised by its bell-shaped capital which is decorated with more than one row of acanthus leaves. It also has four equally-placed small spiral scrolls, and the shaft or column is often un-fluted.

The Composite Order is the most complex of them all, combining grace, strength and ornamentation. The capital is richly decorated with acanthus leaves, scrolls and often other flora and fauna. Similarly, the decoration of the entablatures supported by these five Orders varies sequentially from plain to simple to intricate. Vertical bands give way to more complex dentils and finally to highly elaborate reliefs. These decorations usually appear on the frieze or cornice.

fig 16 CIMS

It is suggested in Morant's "History and Antiquities of Colchester", 1748, that an earlier (Georgian) building stood near the position of the present Grey Friars house. The whole site had passed through various hands and in 1740 it was sold by its owner Thomas Bayes to Dr Robert Potter, who was mayor of Colchester in 1689 and 1700. He therefore probably built a house which may have occupied the site immediately before the present Grey Friars. His portrait in oils, mentioned in his will of 1752 as "by Summers with a rose in my hand", survived (fig 16) and is held by Colchester and Ipswich Museum Services. The issue of whether the previous building was completely demolished, or fell into disrepair, and whether any remnants remain as evidence of a former house, is still to be resolved.

With some architectural knowledge now absorbed, it is time to apply it to the south-facing frontage of Grey Friars (together with Hillcrest) which adjoin the High Street (formerly Frere Street). It is sandwiched between All Saints House (of a similar date) to the east, and Winsley's House, Gate House and East Lodge, all C17th and early C18th buildings, to the west (see figs 2 & 17).

fig 17

The south-facing façade of Grey Friars has an imposing frontage of red brick with two stone string courses running the total length of the building at first and second floor level. This stringing is decorated with miniature moulded corbels on the oldest central section of 1755, but left plain on the later east

100

and west wings. The oldest section is clearly defined but blends architecturally with the later Edwardian wings of 1904. There are 47 sash windows and all but three are of a plain rectangular shape, whereas similar windows in East Hill House opposite have very slight segmental arches (slightly curved at the top). Most of the Grey Friars windows are the 'six over six' design – three panes across by two down for each sliding panel. The older central part of the building, however, has a 'four over four' design, and the second floor has a 'three over three' design. The sash window was one of the greatest inventions of the late C17th and appears again and again in Georgian houses.

Shifting attention to the front door of Grey Friars, it can be seen that the columns either side are of the Ionic order (fig 18). This was considered the order suitable for clergymen and ladies. The columns on either side of the Minories door opposite are only of the Doric order (fig 19). This could be because the Rev John Halls, being a clergyman, was considered to be of a higher social class than the merchant Thomas Boggis of the Minories.

fig 18   fig 19

Returning once more to the Grey Friars doorway, it is evident that the two pillars on either side are not quite free standing, but are attached by a small portion of their shafts to the wall behind. They should therefore be described more correctly as adjoined pillars. These are very similar to pilasters which are a much flatter form of pillar attached to a wall and projecting slightly from it;

101

they are essentially a decorative feature rather than a functional supporting structure. More of these will be seen throughout the interior of Grey Friars, but here, at the doorway, the adjoined pillars do in fact give some support to the entablature with its architrave, plain frieze, and cornice decorated with tooth-like mouldings known as dentils. Above the entablature there is a low-pitched ornamental gable also edged with dentils which is known as a pediment and this is triangular in shape. All these architectural features are shown in figure 20.

Parapet
Pediments
Stringing course

Venetian window

Tympanum

Cornice}
Frieze} ENTABLATURE
Architrave}

Fanlight with tracery
Ionic pilaster or adjoined pillar
Six-over-six sash window

Two-storey bays

fig 20

Often doorways are surmounted by a shallow curve as can be seen again at East Hill House over the road. In both these examples the space formed by the pediment or arch is known as the tympanum which may or may not be decorated in relief. In both these houses they are left blank but the frieze of East Hill House shows ox skulls and flowers in high relief (fig 21).

fig 21

fig 22

The Grey Friars small-roofed doorway space, slightly elevated by three steps, with its pediment above, forms the centre-piece of the Grey Friars south-facing façade, and as such, can certainly be considered a simple portico. Completing this function to impress, there is a glass fanlight above the door with delicate tracery and the name 'Grey Friars' engraved into the glass.

This grandiose front door in the days of the Preparatory and Junior Departments of the Colchester High School for Girls (1920-57) was only for the Headmistress and staff. Pupils used the side entrance behind which a narrow passage with bicycle sheds led to the garden. It was at the extreme end of the east wing adjoining All Saints House (figs 22, 22b and 23).

22b   fig   23

Complementing the pediment over the Grey Friars front door, a second central pediment appears above the first floor window decorated with miniature corbels to match the stringing here. Flanking the door case on either side are a matching pair of two-storey bow windows. This was a deviation from the standard plan of Palladian correctness. John Crunden in his book "Convenient and Ornamental Architecture", 1767, shows a similar house and explains the introduction of the bow windows at the front – "these are more for variety than choice, but a house thus built makes a great figure in the eyes of country people and renders, as they think, the house very cheerful".

The window on the first floor immediately above Grey Friars' front door is of very special interest. It is known as a Venetian or Serliana window. The latter name was derived from the name of the Italian artist and architect Serlio (1475 – 1554) who first illustrated this type of window in his treatise 'Architectura' published posthumously in 1584. He paid great attention to the meanings that different styles could convey, and virtually created a vocabulary to describe aesthetic responses to buildings – but more of this when the interior of this Venetian window is examined.

From the outside this window conforms to the design of a Serliana; it has three parts, the central one arched, wider and taller than the other two. The whole window is supported at its base by four corbels and projects slightly from the verticality of the wall. The two mullions and the left and right borders of the frame are decorated with pilasters of the Ionic order. These are purely decorative and have no supporting function. In the centre of the row of windows on the first floor of the west wing and also the east wing (both added in 1904), a Venetian window has been cleverly copied to continue and balance the neo-classical style of the whole – but neither is so elaborate as the original one over the front door. The Minories also has an C18th Venetian window at the rear facing the garden.

From a position just outside the front door and gazing upwards it is obvious that the east and west wings each have a second storey, whereas the original building of 1755 appears to have only one storey – but the second storey is hidden behind the lower-level parapet.

Connection internally between the four parts of the present building at this height is possible because of the extension to the rear and northwards in 1780 which included a mezzanine floor. Similarly the solid parapet at two levels on the front of the house not only hides and protects the rainwater gullies, but also obscures skylights and small dormer windows which lit the attics and the former servants' quarters. Just visible on the summit is the hipped roof which allows these four separate sections of the building to merge together as one unit.

Finally, it is important to note again that even before Grey Friars was joined to the small house called Hillcrest in 1904, there seems to have been a right-of-way through to the rear of Grey Friars which passed through the interior of Hillcrest. This accounts for the false windows on the first and second floors of Hillcrest above the ground floor window which marks the position of an erstwhile doorway giving entry to this former route (see fig 2 and chapter 4 of part 1 of this book).

3
Ground floor and cellars

From a study of the external features of the south-facing façade of Grey Friars we can now establish that the style of the original building suggests English Palladianism; the style was then copied for the 1904 extension so that all were in harmony with the original concept. The building shows clarity, compactness and restraint. It is very strongly symmetrical and has quite severe and sharp rectangular outlines with undecorated corners. Columns or pilasters only appear on doors and some windows and are never attached to walls. None of the pediments have a broken apex, and the fairly dominant front door is simple, classically-proportioned and correctly detailed. Bearing these features in mind we enter the front door into the outer entrance hall and begin our exploration of the interior (fig 24).

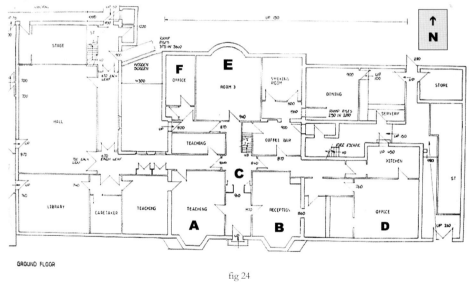

GROUND FLOOR

fig 24

The outer hall is a fairly small space with painted walls and half-panelling to the dado rail. The glass fanlight with tracery above the front door can now be clearly seen (fig 25). Immediately behind the front door as we face northwards, an archway of dark oak leads to the inner hall (fig 26). Arches are reminders of the Roman influence in neo-classical architecture. This archway even has a 'false' decorative keystone which imitates that feature used when stone or brickwork arches are constructed. The key stone in these arches was put in place and while the additional bricks or stones are added and set at an angle to each other, the whole structure is supported by a temporary wooden framework. When this is finally removed the arch has very great weight-bearing properties. This arch and dome building technique using a herring bone pattern has been known since Roman times, and in Renaissance Italy Brunelleschi (1377-1446) designed the massive dome of the cathedral in Florence using no scaffolding. It will have been noticed that the decorative brickwork of the lintels above each of the exterior rectangular windows have no keystone because there is no arch to support.

fig 25

There are identical doors to left and right from this outer hall, both of heavy oak panelling and each one recessed into the wall with the surrounding frame heavily moulded, and each recess bearing its own panelling (fig 27). During the occupancy of the building by the Adult Community College the interspaces on the door frames were painted blue which was consistent with the period in which the house was built. The historic buildings division of the company contracted to redecorate used the pale sky-blue paint which was Robert Adam's choice for the interior of Kenwood House in the 1760s (see appendix) and of course the Grey Friars 1780s extension was built in the Adam style. Above each door frame a row of dentil mouldings are evident and each row is supported at either end by miniature corbels (fig 28). This form of moulding appears again and again throughout the building.

As we progress through the ground floor of the original house built by the Rev John Halls in 1755, the position and function of the various rooms can be clearly seen from the plan in figure 1. The door on the left (west) of the inner hall, for example, led into the Morning Room (A) which would have had the furnishings of the day – Chippendale furniture, painted wallpaper and patterned carpet (exemplified by the room depicted in fig 28b and Appendix).

fig 26 LPP   fig 27   fig 28

fig 28b

The bow window looking out onto the High Street still has its own shutters (fig 29) and the coving, just below the level of the ceiling, is moulded with

107

dentils which are interspersed with moulded flowers. In the days when the building was occupied by Colchester County High School, this was a cloakroom for the Preparatory Department and a classroom when Colchester's Adult Community College took over.

fig 29   fig 29b

fig 30   fig 31

The fireplace surround is a rather dull grey marble streaked with fawn (fig 29b). This is original 1755, apart from the arched cast-iron inset which is circa 1860. The mantel shelf above is supported at each end by an elaborate corbel (fig 30). On either side of the fireplace there is a deep recessed archway, the most westerly one has a door to a corridor behind (fig 31). It is almost certain that this doorway was added when the east and west wings were built in 1904, and that the corridor was originally part of the Butler's Pantry (figure 1).

Returning to the small outer entrance hall, the door on the right (east) leads to an identical room to the one on the left (west). It has a similar shuttered bow window and intricate decorated coving consisting of a mixture of dentils, corbels and moulded flowers (fig 32).

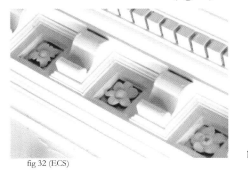

fig 32 (ECS)

fig 33

There is also a splendid fireplace surrounded by black marble with an additional edging of green (fig 33). The mantelpiece is in white painted pine supported at each end by very substantial corbels (fig 33). The front of the mantelpiece is moulded with medallions and vertical grooves.

fig 33

In the days of the Rev John Halls, this was the Breakfast Room (B) and beside the fireplace a two-door hatch leads into the kitchen area behind, as a useful service facility.

It is relevant that during Colchester County High School's occupation this room was a small dining area for the Preparatory Department and for those who had brought packed lunches. It was furnished with low tables and chairs for the smaller children and very different from the furnishing of 1755 where Chippendale chairs might have been in existence.

Moving through the archway from the outer hall to the inner hall (C) we can look back and notice that on either side of the door there is a cupboard with doors which match the door panelling to the Morning and Breakfast Rooms (fig 34). Again the favourite sky blue and white paint of Robert Adam's choice is evident.

fig 34

Turning round, the magnificent main staircase is in front of us (fig 35). It has eleven treads before it bends to the left, then a further five treads until it bends to the left again with a final short flight leading to the landing on the first floor (fig 36). Notice the glass dome above the stairwell which will be given further attention later.

On the right, as the stairs are ascended, the original dark oak panelling which matches the treads still exists (fig 37) On the left, twisting its way upwards, the original banister starts with an ornamental coil - its centre 'eye' probably made of ebony surrounded by ivory (fig 38). The numerous turned oak struts supporting the banister rail present a fascinating climb to the landing.

fig 35

fig 36 ECN

fig 37

fig 38

Sheila Scott remembers her first hours in Grey Friars: "The mini-bar of Cadbury's chocolate we were given after sitting our entrance examination (for CCHS) and the little ebony and ivory 'eye' in the banister rail newel post – which is still there!" Sheila is a wonderful example of someone for whom Grey Friars symbolises important parts of her life. "The hall hasn't changed much at all. We had assembly there every day and I still recall thumping out 'Lily Marlene' on the piano." Sheila has returned to Grey Friars consistently ever since, first as a student of the Music School (now part of Colchester Institute), then as an adult student, and more recently as the pianist, and latterly tutor, of choral classes.

As we pause in the inner hall we notice matching panelled doors to the left and to the right which also again match those to the Morning Room and Breakfast Room which we have already explored. The door to the west leads into a corridor which adjoins the back wall of the Morning Room (fig 39). This corridor only appeared when the 1904 extension was built by the French

111

Nuns. In the Rev John Halls' house it would have been part of a small room to the north which was the Butler's Pantry (fig 1). This plan showing the Butler's Pantry also suggests that the very deep chimney breast would have allowed a fireplace here which was demolished when the west wing was added. The junction of the original 1755 house and the 1904 west wing is clearly visible today. There is a sharp demarcation between the old oak floor boards and a newer marble mosaic floor in black, white and red (fig 40). Here the neo-classical influence is faithfully continued in the black fret border of the mosaic which reflects an ancient Greek influence. At intervals in the mosaic a variation of a Greek cross appears. This religious symbol is very appropriate because the corridor leads to the grand hall, formerly the nuns' chapel where they would have practised their Catholic religion. The double doors which form the entrance to the former chapel can be seen at the end of the corridor.

fig 39   fig 40

Returning to the inner hall, we can now explore what lies behind the door opposite and which appears to lead to the east wing. Again there is a corridor which adjoins the back wall of the Breakfast Room, and so, in effect, this is a mirror image of the first section of the west wing which has just been described. On this dividing wall there is a delivery hatch which backs onto the one already seen in the Breakfast Room. Its position indicates that this corridor only came into being when the east wing was added and was formerly part of the kitchen (fig 1). On either side of the delivery hatch and backing onto the rear wall of the former Breakfast Room there appears to be a void. Part of this is taken up by the large chimney breast, which may also have provided a fireplace here prior to the east wing's construction. Hidden behind some of the flimsy panelling on the western portion is a narrow, dark, servants' staircase. This original staircase had an exit on the first floor and another on the top floor where the servants' quarters were situated. The rest of the void houses a small cupboard and marks the point where the original 1755 building joins the 1904 east wing.

The east wing was built over the former yard which had double gates adjoining the High Street to allow horse-drawn carriages into the Carriage House (fig 1).

At this junction we take a sharp turn to the right and enter a large room with four sash windows looking onto the High Street. This room is in line with the Breakfast Room and has a connecting door. It was used by the Adult Community College as the administrative office. Before that, the French nuns in 1904 may have used it as a workshop, and when they opened their school in 1910 it played a part in the pupils' education. But most certainly when Colchester County High School occupied the building it became the dining room (D) for the Junior Department – and very spartan and disciplined it was too (fig 41). Staff sat at a high table, and enforced silent eating took place. A small hand bell was rung for silence and eating, and then again for talking.

County High School, Colchester, – Dining Hall (Greyfriars)

fig 41

Diana Ruffle and Molly Clarkson (CCHS 1943-48) remember school dinners with menus including tapioca, rice pudding, blancmange and during WW2 brawn and lots of beetroot.

113

Yvonne Watts (nee Goodwin) CCHS 1944-49 remembers the small bell used in the school dining room at lunchtime to signal silence or talking time. She still has it! Her father worked for the Borough Education Office and was involved with the closure of Grey Friars in 1957 when the school moved to its new premises in Norman Way. He rescued the bell before it was thrown away with furniture and other contents left behind when the building was cleared.

Retracing our steps from the dining room back to the position of the original delivery hatch, we see that there is a door opposite this and beyond, an array of back kitchens, larders, storage rooms and sculleries, all of which have been added to and altered over the years to make a network of maintenance areas. When the building came up for sale by Garraways of London on Thursday August 26th 1813, these 'offices' were described as composing "excellent kitchen, store closets, servants' hall, bakehouse and scullery, pantries, larders, dairy and roomy cellars in the basement". All these areas were linked together in the 1980s to form the Refectory of the Adult Community College. Behind a door in one corner of this complex, gloomy twisting steps lead to the cellars (figs 42, 43). These are of great interest because they do not appear to be aligned with the 1755 building and may be a remnant of an earlier house on this site.

fig 42   fig 43

According to an article on Grey Friars, written by Valerie Martin in the Colchester County High School magazine 1946-47 (where she states her sources as John Weaver, Victoria County Histories and Morant) "The dwelling house Grey Friars was built in 1714 when the property was owned by one Thomas Bayes". In addition she notes, "A building on the site of Grey Friars monastery is shown on a plan of Colchester drawn by Pryer in 1724. All that remains today of an earlier building is a four-foot brick foundation wall found when an entry was made from outside into the cellar and the date 1756 on a pipe." This date appears to be the year in which this earlier brickwork was found.

There are numerous adjoining and semi-divided spaces in the cellars, some with arched roofs and doorways, some with racks and one which was obviously cool enough to hang hams and other joints. It has an elaborate door (fig 44) reminiscent of the type used in Iceland and the Faroes today where fish is hung in outside airy spaces and becomes preserved by impregnation with salt from the fierce cold winds blowing off the sea and through the slatted panels. Other remnants of gas lamps, massive pulleys and wine bins also remain (see Appendix). A small derelict fireplace (fig 45) which is almost immediately under the main staircase may have become obsolete when the 1780 north-facing extension was added or may more likely be from a previous building because there now appears to be no chimney stack associated with it.

fig 44   fig 45   fig 46

One section of the cellars through an arched doorway extends under the original yard and has a coal chute for delivery of fuel (fig 46). The area leading up to this section has a very intricate floor (fig 47) and an archaeological examination of this seems to suggest that it contains material which is much earlier than the C18th when the present house was built. This gives credence to the theory that the cellars belong to an earlier house of circa 1714 which either collapsed or was demolished, and may have been built over the cellars of previous structures. Materials from previous buildings and occupations appear again and again as our tour of the site will reveal.

fig 47

The buildings beyond the kitchen, cellars and service areas and surrounding the yard were again described in the Garraway's catalogue of 1813 as a "paved yard with gates to the street, double coach house with a very extensive store-chamber over it and two three-stall stables, brew house and various outbuildings, all of the most substantial brick and of perfect repair". All of these structures extended to within a few feet of All Saints' House next door (fig 1). Most of the yard was later covered over by the large east wing built in 1904, but amongst the hotchpotch of the present interconnecting spaces, a very clear large brick archway with keystone can be seen set into more modern brickwork (fig 48). The best view of this is obtained from the first floor north-facing windows of the east wing. This is undoubtedly the remnant of the wide entrance to the former coach house, but at the time of writing is half-hidden beneath a mid-C20th metal fire escape. This entrance is not aligned with the present frontage of the east wing and suggests that the entrance to the coach house was set back from the road. Within this internal labyrinth of passages, cupboards and small rooms there are arched recesses (fig 49) which speculatively may have been part of harness and tack rooms.

fig 48   fig 49

Retracing our steps once more to the inner hall, a sharp turn to the right (north) past the foot of the staircase takes us to the area immediately outside the Rev John Halls' Dining Room. Here the original 1755 house would have ended with, possibly, a large window looking onto the garden, but the Rev John Halls added the dining room and adjacent rooms to west and east together with matching rooms above on the first floor.

fig 50 BN   fig 51

The extension reduced the light in the inner hall, and to compensate for this a very fine hemispherical glass dome was added in the roof immediately overhead to light the area below (fig 50). This very splendid dome was restored in 1980 but cannot be seen from the outside because it is hidden by the parapet and does not have a drum to raise it sufficiently in order to display its importance. As we look up at the dome from the inner hall we can see that the decoration and mouldings surrounding the circumference of the dome are very intricate. The circle of the dome fits into the centre of an exact square. The perimeter of the square is decorated with carved mouldings, and each corner has a ribbed fan-shaped decoration springing from a cluster of acanthus leaves (fig 51).

The dome and the large extensions to the house were designed and built in the Adam style. Robert Adam himself (1728-92) gradually emerged as an architectural genius after he made a grand tour from 1754-1758, spending some time in Rome. It is therefore fortuitous that the building of the new extension to Grey Friars in 1780 should benefit from these recently-acquired talents. As we visit these later extensions we can contrast the style, decoration and mouldings with those of the earlier part of the house, some of which have already been described in the Morning and Breakfast Rooms.

As we proceed into the Dining Room, one of the most attractive rooms in the house, it is immediately apparent that its neo-classical style and decorations are lighter in relief than the heavier, more robust, Palladian style so easily recognisable in the first part of our tour. This lighter touch is often described as "gaily elegant". And so we step over the threshold of the inner hall to the Dining Room (E). It is immediately striking; airy and lofty, it looks out onto the garden. Its high ceiling is possible because of the mezzanine storey above. It is little wonder in the days of CCHS it was the favourite classroom of all time, even in the 1920s (fig 52).

fig 52

Tables and small chairs together with old-fashioned desks (see Appendix) filled the room. A taller, sturdier desk with a higher chair was set aside for the

118

teacher at the front of the class. Chalk, talk and heavy discipline were the order of the day (fig 52b) which could be relieved by a few surreptitious glances out of the magnificent bow window to the tranquillity of the gardens.

Fig 52b "The Mathematics Mistress" Jean Alexander circa 1936 (see Appendix)

Although the 1780 extension is always described as being built 'in the Adam style', the influence of Robert Adam could, speculatively, have been very first hand. He was certainly in the area in the late 1770s when he was redesigning the old brick-built church at Mistley – some seven miles from Colchester. He finished his work in 1777 and the remaining twin towers can still be seen there (fig 53).

fig 53

Other projects kept him in the area – the Swan Basin and Grapevine Cottages also at Mistley. But by far the most ambitious scheme by a local resident was to turn Mistley into a spa. The Adam style Grecian Salt Water Baths was perhaps one of the best small buildings that Robert Adam ever designed. But it never materialised. The Grey Friars extension, however, came about in 1780.

Devoid of the pupils, staff and furniture, the room has a feeling of opulence. In imagination it is set up for dining in the late 1700s with servants silent and attentive beneath the decorative mouldings and motifs inspired and expanded by Robert Adam who mixed his styles to give his version of neo-classicism a touch of neo-gothic. The mouldings at the cornice in this room are lighter, wider and essentially of low relief. They do not always conform to any strict pattern or design laid down in standard works on mouldings.

One of these mouldings which is a variation on the Vetruvian Scroll moulding shows a scroll growing out of a scroll which is lighter and more feathery than its origin, and is surmounted by a variation on a billet moulding (figs 54a and b). Others appear to have floral or palmette origins. The shallowness and low relief of all the cove mouldings in the room is achieved by using stucco work rather than carved wood. The latter will be seen later when the more robust mouldings of the ornate landing are viewed.

fig 54a   fig 54b AW

It is very sad that the fireplace does not still have its original free-standing cast-iron grate (fig 55). Later, of course, there was additional heating from the old-fashioned Victorian radiators (which can be seen throughout the building) boosted by boilers in the cellars. The immediate surround of the fireplace is a sandy-coloured striated Sienna marble, but the main surround is a pure white very high quality marble with pilasters on either side. This part of the fireplace is original to the room of 1780. The capital of each pilaster is carved with a figure from Greek mythology. The centre (key stone position) is similarly carved.

Few of the many fireplaces throughout the house are completely original with their cast iron grates intact. Others have been altered or added over time to give Victorian or Edwardian flourishes and a few were probably removed during the 1904 alterations and extensions. The Delft tiles lining the back and sides of this Dining Room fireplace were probably added as a decorative feature round about 1900 when the fireplace went out of use. It is unlikely that they are earlier because the blue colours are not strong enough.

fig 55

Interpreting the carved mythological figures on this fireplace is a difficult task. Robert Adam is known to have liked the intrigue of mythology, and figures such as these appear frequently in many of his architectural works. Other fireplaces throughout Grey Friars bear motifs such as swags of flowers and urns carved into the frieze, but nothing so puzzling as these three figures.

The two nude female figures, lightly draped and in low relief on left and right are easy to identify: they are Muses. In Greek mythology, Apollo, God of the Sun was the leader of the nine Muses and their functions are identified from the objects or emblems which they are holding. The Muse on the left (fig 56) is holding a lyre. Both Terpsichore and Erato held lyres, but the former held a large one, and the latter a small one. Terpsichore, however, was nearly always depicted standing rather than sitting, and because she was the Muse of dance and song this seems to fit very neatly into the atmosphere of a 1780s dining room and its after-dinner pleasures. Erato was the Muse of love song and so either of these Muses with their additional weaker association with open spaces (such as gardens) would have been appropriate symbolic choices for this delightful spacious room overlooking the grounds.

fig 56 AW

fig 57 AW

The Muse on the right of the fireplace is unmistakably Euterpe (fig 57), the graceful mistress of song, music, lyric poetry and the inventor of the double flute. She is also the patron of joy and pleasure – and of flute players in general. It is obvious in this relief that music is her main function because she is holding and playing a flute. Again, these are activities which conjure up the ambience of an C18th dining room adjoining the garden.

The central figure in the keystone position appears to be much more important than just a Muse (fig 58). Again, she is a lightly-draped nude with flowing hair and appears to be lying on a rocky surface rather like a sea shore, with gnarled trees beyond. Her arms are thrown up above her head and her facial expression is one of anguish – or is it ecstasy? The carving of this figure is of a much higher quality than the other two and it is quite possible that it may have been executed by a different sculptor, or at a different time, or even that the small rectangle of marble in the centre of the fireplace was added and carved much later – perhaps in Victorian times.

The first possibility is that she represents Ariadne who fell asleep on the beach at Naxos having escaped there with Theseus (who then left for home without her). She sank into deep despair but was soon distracted by the arrival of the festive procession of Dionysus (God of Wine), who fell in love with her and carried her away. The wine theme would therefore fit the dining room. Are the gnarled trees in fact vines?

The second possibility is that this figure represents Andromeda who was chained to a rock as a sacrifice to a sea monster. In this relief a chain is just visible on her right wrist entwined around a rock and this may be acting as a 'marker' so that she can more easily be identified. Amongst the rocks on the right of this relief the head of a 'monster' may just be discernable. In the myth she is seen by Perseus who falls in love with her and enters into a bargain with her father to battle the monster if granted her hand in marriage. This interpretation does not however have the necessary association with wine and pleasure. Both myths are well represented in art. In 1510 Titian painted the arrival of Dionysus meeting with Ariande, and in circa 1515 Piero di Cosimo painted Andromeda chained to a rock. A more recent representation of the latter by Sir Alfred Munnings (who lived in nearby Dedham from 1920 to 1959) was sold in 2013 by Colchester auctioneers Reeman Dansie (fig 58b)

fig 58b RD (see Appendix)

Returning once more to this beautiful former Dining Room, we can see that even more grandeur is added by the bow front with its five tall arched sash windows and entrance to the garden. Robert Adam's predilection for the apse (a semi-circular extension to a rectangular space) perhaps persuaded the C18th designer of Grey Friars' Dining Room to accentuate the curved garden façade in order to give a false sense of spaciousness and mystery - almost akin to that of a Roman bath (fig 59). It lacks a rounded vault above, however. But some features of this magnificent access to the garden can be seen in John Kent's design for Chiswick House in London – the centrally placed low-level double inward and outward opening stable-type doors surmounted by a tall arched window. This unusual architectural feature is sometimes described as a 'window door'.

At each end of the bay is a pilaster - its capital decorated with acanthus leaves. A similar pilaster separates each of the five segments of the bay window. The coving from the top of the pilasters to the ceiling has four rows of different mouldings which in turn are then continuous with the coving of the room (fig 60). Before we retrace our steps to leave by the door through which we entered we have a stunning view of the doorway (figs 61 and 62).

fig 59   LPP

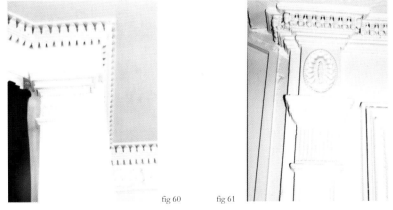

fig 60   fig 61

The immediate door frame has two rows of decorative mouldings separated by plain recessed wood. The innermost moulding shows a string of small flowers, the outer one is a cable-like moulding. The most impressive parts of this doorway are the extremities which show a typical entablature – pilasters either side with capitals supporting an architrave, frieze and cornice and here for the first time we see moulded ornaments called patera (small circular flower-like discs). The central one is circular and the two outer ones are oval (fig 62). The circular patera appear on the metopes of the door surround and are separated by the triglyphs. Many of the mouldings used by Robert Adam are combinations or modifications of the more usual recognised ones, and we will see other examples of this as we proceed.

Fig 62

We exit from the former dining room and enter once again the inner hall. A narrow dark passage on our right with intermittent arched shelving on either side leads westward to a small door opening to the exterior. This would have been part of the former Butler's Pantry – the remainder being behind the left hand wall. In the days of Colchester County High School this latter was a washroom for the younger pupils. Approximately twenty small low-level hand basins joined side-by-side stretched along this north wall. These were removed in the time of the Adult Community College and the space was converted to a small intimate classroom.

On the right, adjoining the small door to the exterior is the entrance to the Rev John Halls' former Library. To the right (east) of this door is the lower section of a narrow staircase (fig 63) which now only leads to a balcony in the Library, but would originally have climbed further as part of a second servants' staircase from the Butler's Pantry to the mezzanine floor. Opposite this is a door surmounted by a semi-lunar window (fig 64) which leads to a lavatory.

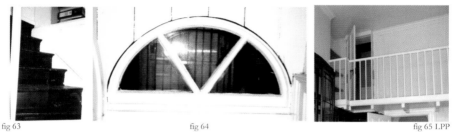

fig 63   fig 64   fig 65 LPP

This once housed a beautiful Victorian lavatory pan decorated with blue flowers and birds (see fig 140). This was still in place when the building was used by Colchester County High School, but was for the sole use of the headmistress, Miss King, whose room was in this former Library (fig 66). Being sent to the headmistress for misbehaviour was a terrifying experience to be avoided at all costs!

County High School, Colchester (Greyfriars)

Fig 66

As soon as the door is opened to the former Library (F) the balcony is the first feature which strikes you, and it becomes obvious that the small section of the servants' staircase which was viewed from outside the entrance also serves the balcony which, it appears, was used for storing books (fig 65).

To light this room there is one Venetian window the frame of which is undecorated. There is a distinctive fireplace with a grey-streaked original white Carrera marble surround. It has a black cast-iron grate and canopy (fig 67). Just above the marble architrave there is a wide frieze carved with swags of flowers and leaves in relief which unite centrally to join a decorative urn (fig 68). This was a very usual symbol for Robert Adam and styles which used his influence. It did not always have funereal connotations, but was more likely to have water-carrying association and was an emblem of the river gods. The tiled inserts on either side date from about 1915.

fig 67

fig 68

As figure 68 shows, the marble cornice just below the mantelpiece is carved with a band of repetitive foliage. It is known that Robert Adam enlarged the repertoire of decorative motifs and mouldings and this may be an example of one of these variations.

On either side of the fireplace built into both alcoves are two full-height mahogany bookcases which were most certainly made to measure and were contemporary with the building of the library in 1780. The top two thirds of each bookcase has glazed panel doors and the lower one third has solid mahogany cupboard doors (fig 69).

We have seen and will see that many features throughout Grey Friars are shared with some of the most spectacular and famous neo-classical buildings in the country. These bookcases are reminiscent of those in the former London home (now a museum) of Sir John Soane (1753-1837). Standard patterns and designs of the day obviously spread their influence from the very grand to the mediocre and finally to the more modest residences.

When the former Library became a headmistress's study in 1920 it was furnished accordingly. The original roll-top desk, armchair, and small side table in the photograph are now held in the archives of Colchester County High School in Norman Way, Colchester. The small rail-back chair by the window was rescued from the attic when Grey Friars was sold in 2008. These items of furniture appear in the Appendix together with an umbrella stand which stood outside this room.

fig 69   LPP

We leave the former library, turn right (westwards) and immediately exit the building by a small door into the garden. Here we shall take a leisurely but observant stroll.

4
Garden Front and grounds

As we exit from the small door to the west and enter a section of the garden, we are confronted by the long wall of the Edwardian wing which extends westward across the former garden. This wing also houses the large hall used as the nuns' chapel. Looking back at the small doorway from which we have just emerged, it is not insignificant although it is only a subsidiary side entrance. It has a pediment and pilasters (fig 70).

Between 1780 and 1900 the house had a variety of owners including clergy and physicians. It is pure speculation that the former library (just to the left of this door) might once have been a doctor's surgery, and the entrance was for his patients so that their activities would be separated from the rest of the household. They would have reached this door by means of the original right-of-way (fig 1). The dark corridor may have been the waiting room – very typical of country doctors' waiting rooms even as late as the 1940s and 50s.

We are now standing in a small sheltered courtyard adjoining this side entrance. During an excavation by Colchester Archaeological Trust in 2004 when the Adult Community College was preparing to have a lift installed to meet the regulations for the use of the college by disabled people, a small section of Roman tessellated pavement was recorded very near to the point where the Edwardian west wing joins the original house extension of 1780.

Today, well above ground, this corner of the original Rev John Halls' house still bears evidence of gardening activities in the late C18th, and this small doorway was more likely to have been for the use of the several gardeners employed to keep the flower borders immaculate. Their tool shed and other associated out-buildings adjoined the west wall of the Library (fig 1). We know from these early plans that there was a lavatory here also. The outline of these varoius structures can be traced on this wall where brick and plaster rendering do not quire marry (fig 71).

This is a more likely explanation for the side entrance which existed to keep the gardeners, their equipment and activities as unobtrusive as possible. Here also, looking upwards we have the first sighting of a cast iron rainwater head with the initials JEH (John and Elizabeth Halls) and the date 1755. (fig 72)

Now out in the open air, a turn to the right takes us into the main part of the garden.

A further turn to the right allows us to pass the Venetian window of the former Library as we arrive at the very large and grand bow window of the former dining room which is slightly elevated above three stone steps (fig 73).

fig 70

fig71

fig 72

This aspect of the building has inspired artists and photographers of all generations. Pupils of Colchester County High School were taken into the garden in summer for their art lessons. And today, in 2014, the immaculate silk screen prints by Julie Graham who chose this building for part of her B.A. degree in Art and Design, emphasise its beauty by linking treasured functional ephemera with prints of the day (fig 74).

fig 73

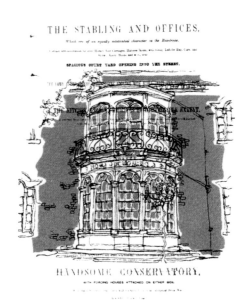

fig 74 JG   fig 75

An overall view of the rear façade of 1780 before the east and west extensions were added shows, like the frontage, that it has a very symmetrical appearance. The double bow windows are flanked on left and right by Venetian windows on both the ground floor and the first storey. The 1904 additions, to some extent, reduce this symmetry but are well hidden so that the whole remains very neo-classical and with its four Venetian windows loses none of its Palladianism.

The large bow window on the ground floor has five arched lights, the central one with an upper sash opening and small low internal and external hinged doors which give access to the garden from the former Dining Room. As we saw earlier when this room was visited, these five lights are separated by highly decorative pilasters. On the first floor, immediately above, the lower bow window is matched by a smaller bow window of three lights. The central one is glazed from top to bottom and forms a pair of doors opening to a small balcony. On either side of these the lights are glazed only in the upper third – the lower part being wood panelling. All three windows, unlike the large arched windows below on the ground floor, have a pointed apex. This is an indication of the Gothic influence which often appeared in the designs of Robert Adam and in houses built in this style.

The two large bow windows and the four Venetian windows, one on either side on the ground floor and one either side on the first floor, are also highly decorated externally with pilasters, medallions and other mouldings (figs 75 and 76). Each pilaster has a shaft and a moulded capital.

Gazing upwards it can be seen that just below the parapet at roof level the stone string course continues, matching that on the frontage. The east and west wings added in the early C20th are clearly visible to left and right but are not obtrusive. Tucked round the corner near the east wing is another rainwater head in a corresponding position to the one just viewed on the west side. It also has the same JEH 1755 inscription. This is more easily viewed from the top floor when we arrive there. The small house known as Hillcrest can just be distinguished on the western side. Originally the two houses were quite separate with a right-of-way and a garden between them – internally we shall see details of this later.

fig 76

The original land attached to Grey Friars when it was a monastery extended as far as the Roman wall, but the walled garden (a car park at the time of writing) was in existence when it was a priory (1904-1920) and remained so as part of Colchester County High School (1920-1957).

Falling away from the garden front with short flights of centrally placed steps between them, there are a series of terraces (fig 77). The upper terrace was originally a badminton court from 1920 immediately after the County High School took over the building. It was a little later marked out as a tennis court.

It was only slightly overshadowed by the ancient Holm Oak. But today there would be no hope of hitting a ball under the canopy of this 400-year-old tree. This tree has a preservation order on it and was placed in the top twelve during a competition run by Colchester's Parks Department in 2008 to find the most impressive and well-loved tree in Colchester Borough.

County High School, Colchester, (Greyfriars)

fig 77

The smaller yew tree on the opposite side of the court – which may be even older – still bears the scars where a wire was tightened round the trunk in order to hold taut the upper edge of a tennis net when it acted as a temporary post. Photographic and cartographic records show that this upper terrace has remained as a lawn for decades, if not centuries.

During the time that CCHS occupied the building the Preparatory and Junior Departments of the school held their sports day on this upper terrace lawn. Ruth Lindsey (CCHS 1939-49) writes "We had team races which included the Bean Bag Race and Tunnel Ball and the individual races included the Egg and Spoon Race, Three-Legged Race and a Sack Race. There would be a gym display and a high-jump contest."

The last occupants to have Grey Friars as a family house were the Fenns (1891-1903) and it is clear from their family photographs that they also used this upper terrace as a tennis court (fig 77b) – and there is also reference (in Part 1 of this book) of croquet being played.

It is easy to speculate that in the C18th a more gentile game of battledore and shuttlecock might have been played here. Equally enjoyed by children and adults, it required no court markings or net and was not even competitive; the sole aim being to keep the shuttlecock going to and fro in the air for as long as possible, and then to record the total, by writing it with quill and ink on the vellum of the battledore together with name and date (see Appendix).

Perhaps this was an after-dinner summer activity enjoyed by the whole family in the late C18th when this medieval game was popular. Chippendale chairs would have been taken from the dining room together with wine glasses and perhaps a blanket to sit on.

Fig 77b

Kate Greenaway produced many illustrations of the game in her children's books of the C19th when the game was still played. But a much earlier engraving (fig 78) shows an adult game in progress with strung battledores rather than vellum ones.

It is interesting to note the outside stairway and raised terrace in the background which would have served as a viewing gallery equivalent to the first storey balcony at Grey Friars. Outside staircases on neo-classical buildings were often a feature at this time as will be discussed later.

fig 78

Another feature of the Grey Friars balcony was that it originally had a lead canopy (fig 79) which would have served to protect the delicate skin of the ladies from the sun – essential for viewing a garden game. Studs holding the canopy in place below the parapet are still visible at the time of writing (2012).

fig 79

Not only would the upper terrace lawn be very visible from the viewing points of the ground floor bay window and the upper balcony but these would also concentrate the gaze on the magnificent conservatory against the southern boundary wall of the garden (fig 80). The conservatory was still in good repair when the Sisters of Nazareth arrived in 1904, but by the 1930s, when Colchester County High School had been in residence for ten years, it was beginning to fall into disrepair. It was known by the pupils as 'the arbour' with its wild and wonderful wisteria winding its way through the ruins. At present nothing is left except for the remains of one or two more unusual shrubs growing against the boundary wall.

County High School, Colchester. (Greyfriars)

fig 80

The Adam style conservatory may not have been built at the same time as the 1780 house extension – it does not appear on the house plans of that era. It was obviously placed against a garden wall because there was no suitable south-facing house wall. It was built when the orangeries in neo-classical

137

houses were beginning to give way to hot-houses and glass palaces. It formed a powerful focal point viewed from the original dining room or balcony with its spectacular glass dome and was reminiscent of the small isolated building called 'The Orangery' in Manhead, Devon or of the grander orangery of Syon House in Middlesex – both designed by Robert Adam.

The lowest and final terrace just in front of the conservatory was tastefully set out with flowerbeds and shrubs and certainly until at least 1920 it was carefully and lovingly tended both by nuns and gardeners (fig 81).

fig 81

Many of the early postcards of Grey Friars which turn up at auctions and postcard fairs were written during the time that the building was occupied by the Sisters of Nazareth or by Colchester County High School, and those that are postally used bear many poignant messages (sometimes in French) sent from England by young novice nuns (or visitors) to their families in France and Belgium. The cards are often of the more picturesque rear of the building or the garden. One example written in French has a small ink cross marked on the first floor western Venetian window (fig 82). It reads "Lots of love to you, little Me'e(?), and to Claude. I've marked our bedroom with a cross." The card is posted in Colchester at 5.45pm on July 24th 1911 and sent to an address in Paris (fig 82b). The census forms of the day indicate that one of these girls was a 15-year-old (Marguerite Rameau) who might have been a pupil boarding at the nuns' school in 1911, or even a novice nun in training.

fig 82 (above)

fig 82b (below)

Another card, again in French, which may have been from one of the nuns, was posted on April 2nd 1906 to Belgium and signed by Sheila reads, "My very dear Marthe for a long time I have wanted to write to you, but I did not have the time from one Sunday to the other, and time has passed. Milly, without a

139

doubt, has said to you that I will not return at Easter, but I am sure that the time that I will spend here in England will be very pleasant and interesting – doubtless it will include several little journeys and we will spend a day in London. There will always be plenty to do. I would be very happy to receive all your news. Friendly memories, Sheila." Maybe a small pocket rosary found under the Grey Friars floorboards (see Appendix) belonged to one of the child boarders or to a nun who looked after them, or even again a novice nun.

Returning to the conservatory which was obviously a centre of great interest, admiration and attention, we move eastwards from it and along the red brick boundary wall where we find that there is a small pedestrian gate leading into Castle Road (fig 83). Nearby there used to be a small pond providing the pupils of Colchester County High School the fascination and excitement of watching the newts and water snails which were beyond their reach – or of falling in! The remainder of this high wall is of red brick as also is the east garden wall which separates the grounds of Grey Friars from Roman Road.

County High School, Colchester.- Playground. (Greyfriars)

fig 83   fig 84

Despite repeated repairs, replacement and general refurbishment particularly the southern wall with its preservation order, all the walls continue to provide shelter for wild life, and footings for some attractive native wall plants which spring up in its crevices. The most notable of these is ivy-leaved toadflax – which is becoming rare. At the time of writing lesser celandines and comfrey grow in profusion on the ground near the pedestrian gate, grey squirrels inhabit the Holm Oak, and an occasional pair of mallards fly in from the Castle Park.

Within the right angle made by the junction of the north and east boundary walls there was, in the days of the County High School, an asphalt playground with netball courts marked out (fig 84). The late Margaret Sherry Podgorska (CCHS 1930s) wrote "At playtime tops and yo-yos were much in evidence in the large asphalt playground".

Magnificent fragrant flower borders were separated from this area by a high netting fence with a raised path running from west to east (fig 85). An ancient pear tree (on the right) used to shed its hard fruit onto the path in early autumn.

During World War 2 air raid shelters replaced some of the flower borders and were even constructed close to the mighty Holm Oak. Excavations by Colchester Archaeological trust have revealed traces of these. At the time of writing this whole area is now a car park (fig 86), the upper and lower areas separated by a low privet hedge. This hedge follows approximately the same line as the raised pathway alongside former flower borders, and it had a small summer house at the eastern end for the amusement of the school pupils. Prior to this when the French nuns occupied the building before 1920, a crucifix was in this same position. The exact site can be pinpointed from two chimneys of houses which still exist in Roman Road (fig 87).

fig 85

fig 86

Ruth Lindsey (CCHS 1939-49) writes "Air raid shelters were long tunnel-like places with wooden benches along the sides and, right at the end, the Elsan-type toilet. In the early days of 1940/41 we were often sent scurrying across the playground by the air-raid siren, all clutching our gas masks and emergency rations to spend a somewhat cold and musty-smelling time waiting for the 'all-clear' to sound.

Christine Mabbit (CCHS 1926-38) recalls that there was also a mulberry tree which fell in a storm whilst she was there. No doubt during its life this was one of the sources of mulberry leaves fed to silkworms reared by pupils at CCHS during the school's early days. Delia Bloom (CCHS 1940s) remembers "Rounders was the outside sport. We played at the far end of the playground, and I remember one day a girl getting her finger stuck in a hole in the wall during a game; and it is just recently that I discovered the identity of that girl – Joan Gurney." She had become bored awaiting her turn to bat and had decided to explore the crevice – a flint with a hole in it.

The boundary wall to the south, separating the grounds of Grey Friars from the garden of All Saints House was once (certainly in Colchester County High School days) a very fine flint wall with interesting shaped stones some with holes in them – very attractive to little fingers of the Preparatory Department.

fig 87

Against the eastern wall separating the grounds of Grey Friars from Roman Road were small individual gardens for each child.

Joan talks to Beth Chatto OBE:
Beth was born Betty Diana Little in 1923 and entered the Junior Department of CCHS when she was 12 years old, staying till the sixth form which was with the senior department at North Hill (where the Sixth Form College is now based).

"This building did not have the same feeling and aura of Grey Friars which was special," she said. "I had an individual garden at Grey Friars, as did other pupils. These small gardens adjoined the wall which separated the playground from Roman Road. A pathway ran alongside, edged with apple trees. We, the pupils, grew mainly annuals and we used to spend a few pence on packets of seeds at Woolworth's. It may not have been apparent at the time, but I think the seeds of my future career germinated in these little gardens. Although I was an enthusiastic gardener, I never realised that I would become a professional one. My parents were passionate about their garden and so I grew up with this all around me. Initially, I trained as a teacher during the War."

Beth remembers the magnificent Grey Friars flower borders, the ancient Holm Oak and the black mulberry which supplied leaves for the many silkworms which the pupils kept in

142

cardboard boxes. But the imposing conservatory had, by her time, completely disappeared. When I asked her which part of the house interior was her favourite, she replied, "It was the entrance hall and the view of the main staircase from inside the front door – the long sweep of the stairs, the polished handrail and the wooden flooring." She did also admit to sliding down the bannisters!

She also remembers a younger pupil, Pamela Brown, who became a famous children's author (see Appendix), Miss Ruth King the Headmistress, a strict disciplinarian – and Latin lessons. How useful these latter were to be to her in her study and interpretation of plant names and the manner in which she explains them so clearly to others. "And how useful to everybody else," she declared, "in their understanding of the origin and structure of words."

When I asked her if gardening shaped the human personality characteristics of patience, tolerance and caring, she replied that, thankfully, all great gardeners are different, but good gardeners look, see and understand what plants require. Her philosophy she said, was one of caring for plants, knowing their needs, placing them correctly and giving them a habitat that is ecologically suitable. "If they thrive in sun, give them sun. If they like shade, give them shade. Plants, over thousands of years, have adapted to survive in many different conditions, and by learning which these are, we can find suitable ones to help us transform problem areas in our gardens."

I asked if she had painted or written creatively when she was at CCHS and she replied, "My plants are my art, not always for their colour but for their shape, form, texture and behaviour. I arrange my plants as an artist arranges his picture to create a natural look. I use the influence of the Japanese Asymmetrical Triangle – heaven is vertical, earth is horizontal and falls away, and man is in between."

As we discussed the subject of art, we moved on to the friendship which Beth and her late husband, Andrew, developed with Cedric Morris, the artist who, with Lett-Haines, founded the East Anglian School of Painting and Drawing at Hadleigh in Suffolk.

"We were friends for over 30 years," she said. "He opened my eyes with his glowing colours and textures, and of course he was a gardener of renown and inspired me. In the early days, Andrew and Cedric seemed to know all the Latin names, but by regular checking and handling plants, I soon caught up. Cedric introduced plants into cultivation which were not commonly found except in the wild. Many of my plants originally came from him. At that time, we all enjoyed a culturally rich atmosphere, talking about plants, gardening, music, architecture, painting and civilised living."

And then, with a little smile of nostalgia and reverting to our earlier conversation, she concluded, "The school we went to was a good school. We [you and I] were so lucky to go there."

An occasional brick buttress helped to support the southern wall. It was replaced in the 1960s by one made of less attractive concrete blocks. However, a fine shrine also made of flint was set into the original wall and still survives as a relic of the nuns' occupation. It is however becoming increasingly obscured by rampant ivy (fig 88). Originally framed by flowering climbers and a backdrop of St James' Church with its Gothic windows, on the opposite side of the road, the shrine's position can be reliably fixed today (fig 89).

fig 88   fig 89

All the boundary walls of Grey Friars have stories to tell, and as we proceed westwards along the southern wall we come to one of the most intriguing sections close to the original stable block (fig 90). After a small part behind this collapsed in the 1990s an analysis of a barrow-load by Colchester Museum Services clearly pointed to Roman elements in its composition.

Passing the impressive garden front of Grey Friars once more we come to the western boundary wall. This is the most interesting wall of all. It is a conglomerate of brick, tile, stone, flint and cement - some elements of it may be mediaeval and some Roman. It was obviously put together from the remains of previous buildings which may have been strewn across the site. At regular intervals along it, red brick structures, although flush to the wall, may be acting as buttresses (fig 91).

At the southernmost end of the wall nearest to Grey Friars house a small pointed doorway and matching door lead into a space behind, which in the days of Colchester County High School was the gardener's shed and later was Colchester Adult Community College's kiln room used by ceramics classes (fig 92). The pointed arch here of Gothic design may go back some way. A small drawing of 1718 (included in part 1) shows the remains of Grey Friars monastery with several Gothic archways. The original monastery is thought to have been much further to the east of the present building (almost opposite St James church) but there is always speculation that this existing doorway was in the same position as an earlier Gothic structure. At the site of this doorway the western wall takes a sharp dogleg bend to the west in order to encompass the site of the original side garden and right-of-way, and then is discontinued (see section 1).

fig 90

fig 91

At the northernmost end of this wall before it meets the southern boundary and the original conservatory there is another small overgrown shrine (fig 93) of brick and stone – an additional clear piece of evidence pointing to the use of the building as a priory. Again, this shrine would have contained a statue of the Virgin Mary during the nuns' occupation.

fig 92

fig 93

Our guided tour of the grounds of Grey Friars cannot end without referring to the layout and contents of the Botanic Gardens. In January 1824 the Botanical Society of Colchester announced that it had leased land opposite St James' church on East Hill (described by the Ipswich Journal of 1823 as 'rich meadowland') with the intention of forming a botanical garden. This would have been the land lying in the north-east inner corner of the town, the Roman/Medieval town wall forming the north and east boundaries and the southern boundary bordering High Street. It was approximately 8.5 acres

The Botanic Garden covered the site of the present Roman and Castle roads. (Further details of this venture can be found in section 5 of part 1 of this book.) Grey Friars itself was in an elevated position, and the gardens fell away towards the Roman wall, surely providing a spectacular vista.

Excavations along the northern section of the town wall according to P.M. Duncan in "The History and Description of the Walls of Colchester" revealed an underlying 'dark tunnel'. Although no evidence of these gardens nor the 'dark tunnel' remain today, there was certainly a myth elaborated by the girls of Colchester County High School in the 1930s that somewhere in the grounds of Grey Friars there was a secret tunnel (for purposes unknown) which led to Colchester Castle, or even perhaps, to St James' church.

Diarist and antiquarian William Wire notes on a plan of 1847 that any monastic fragments remaining after apparent demolition of the monastery were later salvaged and used for ornamentation. Pencil drawings by Josiah Parish from the late 1840s (figs 94 to 99) capture the tranquillity and diversity of the gardens and show them to be large and picturesque with naturalistic sculptures, trellis work, fish ponds, shrubberies, grottoes, walkways and avenues. If, as we explored in chapter 5 of section 1 of this book, the present high wall was not built until after the closure of the Botanic Gardens, these sights must have provided a pleasing outlook for the residents of the Grey Friars house during this period. The whole site was tastefully laid out (fig 100) and had an integrated nursery to help with the running costs. This figure is from the catalogue prepared in 1847/8 for the sale of the Botanic Gardens. The labels added by Julie Wilde for her book "The Botanic Gardens of Colchester" have been augmented by the authors.

The public attraction of the Botanic Gardens fluctuated. In 1849 the site was disposed of in its entirety to the National Freehold Land Society (with stock included). By 1852 it had become Roman and Castle roads with small plots laid out for building purposes.

figs 94-99 Josiah Parish drawings of the Botanic Gardens (CIMS)

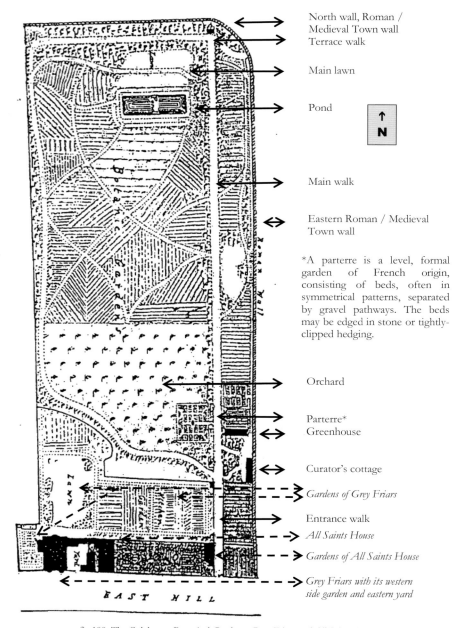

North wall, Roman /
Medieval Town wall
Terrace walk

Main lawn

Pond

Main walk

Eastern Roman / Medieval
Town wall

*A parterre is a level, formal
garden of French origin,
consisting of beds, often in
symmetrical patterns, separated
by gravel pathways. The beds
may be edged in stone or tightly-
clipped hedging.

Orchard

Parterre*
Greenhouse

Curator's cottage

Gardens of Grey Friars

Entrance walk

All Saints House

Gardens of All Saints House

*Grey Friars with its western
side garden and eastern yard*

↑
N

EAST HILL

fig 100 The Colchester Botanical Gardens, Grey Friars and All Saints House

148

It was the end of the Botanic Gardens, and sadly, they left no trace of their former glory for present-day observers to enjoy. The site, which once provided a spectacular vista from Grey Friars' elevated position, looking down towards the town wall, and had acted as a place of recreation, enjoyment and more importantly a place of education for the public, was abandoned and sold.

An extract from an 1890s guide book to Colchester chimes with the ethos for our book. This corner of Colchester may be ignored and unknown by some but holds nostalgic memories and pleasurable experiences for many. Its full story therefore has to be told. Dr P.M. Duncan wrote: "The quiet nook loved by Celt, Roman and solitary Friar, which heard the death volley of glorious Lucas, and which is sacred to many a happy memory in later days, now belongs to a Freehold Building Society redolent of shares and £10 voters, the quietest part of the quietest corner being used as a burial place for Quakers."

A certain sense of déjà vu existed however when Colchester County High School for Girls arrived some thirty years after this guide book was published. The aims of the Botanical Society were to set out collections of all classes of plants with a classified arrangement for the use of students of botany. Plants would be labelled in English and Latin and the gardens would include fruit trees, shrubs, forest trees and aquatic plants. This legacy of Latin, Botany and Gardening, which had given the area its association with learning, was instilled into the new occupants from an early age. Records exist showing the pupils' interest in the natural world around them. Trees, plants and flowers were depicted in charcoal, crayon and paint. Animals were closely observed and flowers were pressed (fig 101). A ten-year-old in 1942 drew seeds and fruits in her exercise book (figs 102/3). The same ten-year-old then filled her nature notebook with the life histories of birds and animals. Many of these examples would have been taken from the grounds and pond of Grey Friars itself.

figs 101-3

149

As we continue our tour of the grounds of Grey Friars, it is vital to remember that what lies underground may be equally as important in tracing the lives of others who have occupied the site.

At the completion of our walk around the Grey Friars grounds we can now visualise that the friary cemetery would have been the upper portion of the eastern car park. The plan of the Botanic Gardens also shows a very important square, landscaped area (which was the parterre) and was easterly from the house itself. This was very similar to the remains of a cloister in an earlier sketch by William Stukeley (1718) (see part 1 of this book, section 4) which could place the monastic church on the south side of the cloisters. The discovery of part of the burial ground in the former kitchen garden (now part of the car park adjacent to the garden wall of All Saints House) would confirm that it was next to the church. This close proximity of church and cloisters was the usual arrangement in a monastic community.

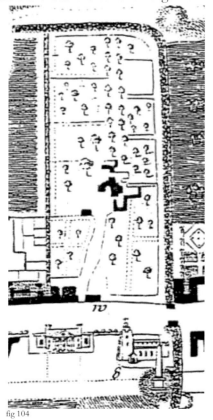

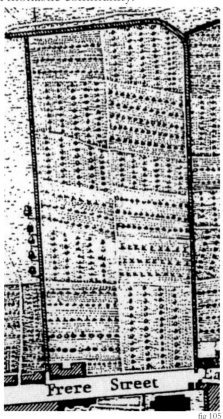

fig 104

fig 105

We have now finished our tour of the grounds of the present Grey Friars, both above ground and below ground and we return once more to the magnificent garden front. We leave behind in our imagination the sounds, scents and sights of gardens past, the shadowy figures of friars and nuns going about their religious devotions and the happy voices of schoolchildren playing marbles and hopscotch. We enter and pass through the former Dining Room to the inner hall where we will pause before climbing the staircase to the first floor.

5
The first floor

In the inner hall we look upwards to the hemispherical dome which drenches the inner hall with light – added, as we already know, to provide this light after the original Dining Room was added by the Rev John Halls in 1780. We ascend the wide staircase with its two bends to the left and we admire once again the impressive balusters on the left and the equally magnificent oak panelling on the right. As we step onto the main landing (G) we are experiencing what perhaps is the most lavish piece of decoration in the whole of this neo-classical building. We face the Venetian window which looks out onto the High Street, flanked by adjoining rooms. Our backs are towards the 1780 mezzanine floor with its delightful central balcony room overlooking the garden. The rest of the relatively plain first floor rooms of 1904 fall away from the corridors to east and west adjoining this original highly-decorative landing (fig 106).

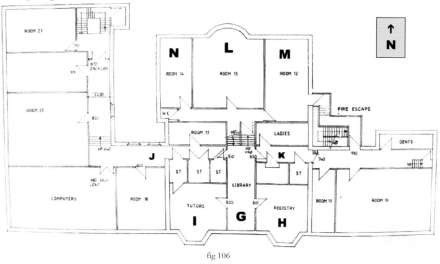

fig 106

We are surrounded by classical mouldings of every type – around doorways, coving, panelling, and of course the central Venetian window. It is difficult to imagine that this richly-decorated space was only the landing of a 1755 house. It might have fulfilled another purpose. In Garraway's sale of August 1813 the house is described as having "seven airy bedchambers on the first storey with storeroom, closets etc." Two of these lead off the landing, have windows to the front and are also heavily decorated – unusual for bedrooms. (H and I).

Two more, plainer, ones are now indistinguishable having been absorbed by the east and west extensions made in 1904. Both of these, as with all bedrooms of this period, would have had fireplaces, which, of necessity were removed to make way for the corridors to the east and west (J and K). The other three bedrooms occupy the mezzanine floor.

Another reference in a paper attributed to the late Enid Bishop, a former Principal of the college, states that the contrast in styles between some plainer rooms on the ground floor and some more decorative ones on the first floor suggest that the clergyman (the Rev John Halls) occupied the plainer rooms and his wife and mother-in-law occupied the more decorative ones. But this model does not seem to fit.

It is tempting to speculate that this relatively large landing with its four adjoining bedrooms was a "piano nobile" which would have been copied from a Palladian building of the Renaissance period where the first floor, and its rooms, were a reception area for guests. This would explain the lavish decorations which were to impress the guests. Against this theory is the fact that there is no external cascading stairway. This was a very important feature in Palladian style buildings (such as Chiswick House in London which has an exceptional example) to allow access to the first floor reception area without passing through the mundane ground floor and servants' quarters.

Whatever the reason behind this exceptionally decorative landing, it can still be admired. There are mouldings of many types and several that are very typically favoured by the Victorians. Most of these are carved wood in contrast to those in the Adam style already seen in the ground floor Dining Room which were mostly of plaster and gesso. Above the oak panelling of the staircase is a moulding known as 'running dog' (fig 107). Oak panelling to the dado rail would have continued around all the walls of the landing (fig 108).

fig 107

County High School, Colchester. (Greyfriars)

(above) fig 108

Oak would also have been used to frame the doorways. At the time of writing the panelled doors and surrounds have been picked out (during the 1980s) in blue and white which lighten the effect (fig 109). These were the favourite pale sky blue and white of Robert Adam's choice (see Appendix). In the 1700s, also, many of the mouldings would have been emphasised with lavish gold leaf. Others would have been left in their natural dark oak state. The mouldings around all four doorways leading off the landing follow an ordered

154

scheme. Egg and dart (another favourite Victorian moulding) appears around all of them (fig 110). Additional mouldings include those known as bead, cable, wave and dentil (see Appendix).

110 fig 111

The intricacies of the carvings around the Venetian window are quite exceptional (fig 111 and 111b). At least two more types of mouldings can be distinguished here and corbels make an additional decorative feature (fig 112).

fig 111b

fig 112

They surmount the two carved sections which separate the arched central portion of the window from the two flanking rectangular sections. Here the attention to detail and meticulous carving almost stop us in our tracks. The two panels are individually worked and far from matched, neither are they mirror images. They are not intended to be (figs 113, 114).

Twining stems, foliage and flowers are rich and lifelike – much in the manner of Grinling Gibbons (1648-1721). He was a leading English sculptor who not only worked in marble, stone and bronze, but was much more famous for his

155

decorative carvings in wood – particularly limewood – which were delicately executed as ornament for panelled interiors, picture frames, overmantels, choir stalls and screens (such as those in St Pauls' Cathedral). Several of his contemporaries and those who followed on after him were heavily influenced by his designs and techniques, and it is possible that the sculptor of these Venetian window carvings was touched by his genius. This interesting landing in the days of the Adult Community College was, for a period of time, a library, where the motifs around could be as stimulating as the words in the books themselves. In contrast, when the building was occupied by Colchester County High School, the space under the Venetian window was the sick bay, with the bed head immediately underneath the window - facing it with its intricate beauty would surely have produced instant recovery!

fig 113

fig 114

fig 115

Continuing our tour, a panelled door to the east with its surrounding egg and dart mouldings and scroll and leaf decoration above leads to a highly decorated room (H), which in the days of the Adult College was the Registry. Whether it was the master bedroom of the original house or an elaborate reception room designed to impress is again a matter for speculation. In shape and size it reflects the room below. All window and door surrounds and coving are lavishly decorated with egg and dart and dentil mouldings. The bay (fig 115) with its three sash windows, shutters and shelves exactly matches those of the Breakfast Room on the ground floor.

The most outstanding features of this room are the overmantel and the fireplace. (fig 116). The overmantel appears to be original and includes a mirror which reflects light back into the room. It is very like the overmantel in the watercolour in fig 28b which illustrates the furnishings of a morning room of the late 1700s. This gives added credence to the fact that this room on the first floor was far too impressive to be just a bedroom.

fig 116

The decorative pine surround of the mirror (which almost extends to the coving of the ceiling) is exquisitely carved with vine leaves and bunches of grapes which hang in full ripeness down both sides of the frame (figs 117/18). Each side of the mirror, like the Venetian window decoration, is not matched and quite independent. The grandness of the over-mantel overshadows the fine mouldings of the coving in this room. Here we have the usual dentils and below this a variation of egg and dart around the entire circumference of the room (fig 119).

fig 117

fig 118

fig 119

fig 120

The fire grate in cast iron has moulded acanthus leaves and other floral designs and is almost certainly original and contemporary with the period of the room (fig 120). This in turn is surrounded by pink-striated marble raised into concentric ridges. This has an additional wooden surround which is elaborately carved. At the time of writing these carvings (fig 121) cannot be clearly distinguished because unfortunately in the days of the Adult Community College they were covered over with red paint together with the mantelshelf and its fine supporting corbels.

We now return to the landing and explore the room on the western side of the Venetian window (I). In the Adult Community College, this was the Senior Tutors' room, and we will now assume that it was bedroom number two in 1755.

fig 121

We find again, that it is identical in size and shape to the room below it on the ground floor – the Morning Room. It is also very similar to the master bedroom (H) which we have just left - but it lacks the luxurious details and extensive decorations. The bow window is similar with small seats below. The only significant decorations are the dentils around the coving. As we turn round to face north the fireplace is seen to be relatively simple with a cast-iron undecorated grate either side of which is a single vertical row of rose-coloured tiles. The whole is surrounded firstly by black marble and then by a pale grey mottled marble with matching mantelshelf. This is a fireplace that has been adapted at a later date (fig 122) – probably in Victorian times.

fig 122 LPP   fig 123

Unlike the master bedroom, however, either side of the fireplace there is a door, and each door leads into a cupboard space on either side of the chimney breast. One of these cupboards (on the west side) has an additional door leading out from the back (fig 123). The one on the eastern side would

159

also have once had a door at the back. The whole of this chimney area and two cupboards would have originally backed onto bedroom number three in the Rev John Halls' house, the two cupboards perhaps acting as closets – one to each bedroom. Here the occupants of each bedroom could retire to pray, look at paintings, study, meditate in solitude or store away treasures. But by the time that this house was built, closets were becoming redundant. In the present building, at the time of writing, we have to imagine this because of the west wing added in 1904 which took part of this bedroom to make a corridor running westwards.

Leaving this bedroom and entering the landing again, we return to the top of the main staircase. Opening the door on the left with its matching decorated surround, on the west side of the landing, we see a corridor (J). This corridor firstly leads to an archway. This archway marks the point where the 1904 extension began and would originally have been part of the space of bedroom three – the rest of the room being made up by the small room on our right - the opposite side (north) of this corridor. There was a bedroom fireplace between two cupboard doors which was removed during the extensions westwards in 1904. The two doors at the rear of the cupboards of bedroom two can be clearly seen in fig 124 which is looking back (eastward) towards the door we have just entered from the landing, which would originally have been the bedroom door.

fig 124

fig 125

Turning around again and looking through the archway leading westwards (fig 125) is the corridor (J) again which forms part of the newer west wing built on by the French nuns in 1904. Two doors are in the distance on the left; the first leads into a small room with two sash windows, and the second into a larger room with three windows (fig 126); one of these is a 1904 copy of a Venetian window which allows the frontage of the building to be in keeping with the original neo-classical style of the C18th. No elaborate decorative mouldings exist either on the inside or outside of this window, but the three sections of the false Venetian window are enclosed, as can be seen in the photograph, by an archway in relief. During the time the Adult Community College occupied the site this room was a spacious computer room.

126 fig 127

Outside this room, just discernible from our new viewpoint, a flight of six steps rises at right-angles to the western corridor. This takes us into a further short corridor with three rooms on the immediate left (west), see fig 106. These steps with the elevated cluster of rooms give added height to the large original chapel which the nuns added on the ground floor below us. This was later used as a hall for both school and college gatherings. But we shall have a further detailed look at this area towards the end of our tour.

Returning to the top of the main staircase again and looking through the door which leads to the corridor to the east (K) it is obvious that this is an almost exact mirror image of the other corridor (J) and its adjacent rooms. Exactly the same situation exists here. The doorway seen in fig 127 marks the point where the new east wing was built in 1904, and this first section of the corridor forms part of bedroom number four which backs onto the chimney breast of the master bedroom number one, and would have also included the small room on the left (a block of toilets in school/college days). It also, as a bedroom, would have had a fireplace, later removed by the nuns to accommodate the new east wing.

161

It is now time to explore this initial small section of the east wing corridor (K). As we enter the first part of the corridor (originally part of bedroom four) we notice immediately that there are some interesting features on the right-hand wall which backs onto the master bedroom number one. It is obvious that these do not just conceal a large void behind the panelling. Firstly, the chimney of the master bedroom occupies the majority of this space but the panel on the nearest side to the landing has a very hollow sound when tapped, and opening the inset door we discover that the servants' narrow twisting staircase from the ground floor is accessible here, and that it continues upwards to the second floor and downwards to the ground floor (figs 128 and 129).

The rest of this space around the chimney breast is occupied by a store cupboard, but immediately in front of the chimney there is a large metal handle and a slot which resembles a letter box (fig 130). As this is immediately above a similar structure on the ground floor we can speculate that it was, in the Rev John Halls' day, a type of dumb waiter which must have continued to the second floor above and the servants' quarters. There is also a flue here to the large chimney stack which may have been to assist the sweeping process of the two back-to-back fireplaces.

fig 128   fig 129   fig 130

131 fig 132

The rooms to the south of this eastward-running corridor are exact mirror images of those in the west wing. A small room on the right has a sash window facing the High Street and the next larger room has a matching false Venetian window similar in dimensions to the one in the west wing. Again, the three sections of this window are enclosed internally by a decorative archway in relief (fig 131).

On the opposite side of the corridor to this room, a sash window facing the garden gives a good view below of the remains of the large archway which may mark the entrance to an original coach house and has already been seen on the ground floor. At the eastern extremity of this corridor we come to a narrow oak staircase to the second floor which we will examine later.

We return once more to the landing and facing north we notice that a short flight of six steps takes us to the mezzanine floor nicely illustrated in fig 108 as it was in Colchester County High School's day. This short flight of steps with oak balusters and hand rail matching those of the main staircase which we climbed earlier, leads to a small landing (fig 132). This was the upper storey to the 1780 extension added by the Rev John Halls. It was raised as a mezzanine floor to give extra height to the imposing Dining Room below, and its flanking Library to the west, and the kitchen and scullery areas to the east. The narrow landing at this level has three rooms opening from it and these were perhaps bedrooms five, six and seven. All the mouldings around these doorways copy the design of those in the rooms below and have a lighter more delicate touch typical of the Adam style.

If we pause at the top of the six steps and look backwards and upwards we see an unusual feature at the level of the second floor. Here an arched, glazed doorway, protected on its lower half by an oak balustrade, conceals a cast-iron furniture hoist (fig 133).

fig 133 LPP

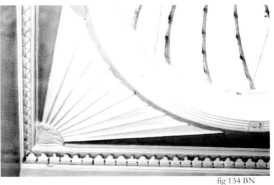

fig 134 BN

This was obviously in position before the 1780 extension and was used to hoist large pieces of furniture to the first and second floors. Just below it as a decorative feature a fine piece of running dog moulding in dark oak completes the picture. Here also we get a closer and very fine view of the underside of the dome with its mouldings and fan-shaped decoration springing from a cluster of acanthus leaves (fig 134).

The centre room on the mezzanine floor (L) has as its entrance a pair of double-panelled doors with delicate fern-shaped mouldings on either side (fig 135). The whole doorway is surmounted by an enormous moulded shell-shaped fan (fig 136). Entering this centre room it is immediately obvious that the external doorway mouldings are more elaborate than the internal features. There are no mouldings at the coving or dado rail, and very sadly at some stage between 1956 when the County High School left and 1966 when adult education took over, the fireplace was robbed out. All that remains is a pale marble surround suggesting that at an earlier stage something more elaborate had existed. Certainly former pupils of CCHS from the 1920s and 30s can recall having fire-stoking duties when an open fire was used for heating the room. The size of this room however is impressive - very slightly smaller than the former Dining Room below it on the ground floor. Double full-length glazed doors occupy the centre of the bow window and are flanked on each side by a smaller half-height window. The central glazed doors open onto a balcony which runs externally round the full extent of the bow. These three windows seem contradictory to the main style of the house for they are pointed in the Gothic style with a hint of tracery at the apex. The Gothic phase was a C14th form of architecture but was popular in the C19th when there was a vigorous revival. The Robert Adam style in which this extension was built in 1780 did however use elements of Gothic architecture to lighten the neo-classical features (fig 137). Robert Adam was also very fond of 'ribbon' mouldings in some of his internal features as in fig 138 which shows the decoration on the edges of the ground floor former library's fireplace.

figs 135   fig136   fig137

The external balcony has a balustrade made of scrolled wrought iron and suggests again that this grandeur is more in keeping with a reception room of a 'piano mobile' which may have acted as a viewing area for the garden and the activities on the lawn below, rather than just being a bedroom. This room was used as the bursary of the Adult Community College.

Leaving this room and walking down a short corridor to the west under an archway, the door in front of us (with a window over) leads into a lavatory (fig 139). In the days of Colchester County High School there was a Victorian lavatory pan here decorated with blue flowers and birds similar to the one already described previously in the identical space immediately below on the ground floor. A similar one is displayed in the Dick Joice Museum at Holkham Hall, Norfolk (fig 140).

fig 138   fig 139   fig 140 DJM   fig 141

Christine Mabbitt remembers "a lavatory with an enormous toilet – I was afraid of falling in. All the toilets were wonderful pieces of ceramic with wide wooden seats."

She recalls the view from "beautiful bay windows opening onto the terrace" and the impressive trees (oak, yew, walnut, lime, chestnut) many still in situ. "The eucalyptus seems to have disappeared. The mulberry fell down in a storm while I was there and the big beech was removed to make the back entrance of the clinic. The conservatory with its gigantic sweet-smelling wisteria went for the same reason." She echoes many others' views: "It was a beautiful place in which to be educated. The atmosphere of the building and the large garden left an indelible impression."

The panelling in this area of the mezzanine floor again has a hollow sound which would seem to indicate that the narrow staircase outside the former Library below, and which appeared to end at the height of the Library balcony, in fact once continued to the mezzanine floor and was perhaps a second servants' service staircase from the Butler's Pantry which once occupied the space over the spot where the Victorian toilet was added. Another bedroom closet may also have been here.

165

The door to the north adjoining the lavatory leads into bedroom number six. This is the same size as the room below and was the Vice-Principal's room in the Adult Community College (N). It has an identical Venetian window to the Library undecorated on the inside, but decorated with pilasters on the outside (fig 141). There are few mouldings in this room, but the fireplace flanked by cupboards with panelled doors each side is the most distinguishing feature although it lacks its cast-iron grate (fig 142). It has a surround of white marble and the architrave is carved with very typical Adam style designs. A carved urn in the centre, similar to the library, supports two carved floral swags attached to carved supports at each end (fig 143). Again, during adult college days, the cupboard doors were picked out in Adam-style sky blue and white.

(above) fig 142   (below) fig 143

The final bedroom (M), which is number seven, is at the east end of the mezzanine floor, slightly larger than bedroom six but decoratively almost identical. This was the Adult Community College's Principal's room. It has a

Venetian window identical to bedroom six (fig 144) and a fireplace of the same size. It is immediately over the kitchen and scullery areas on the ground floor. The fireplace surround is of black marble, but the back plate and grate have long since disappeared (fig 145). Below the mantelshelf is a central white marble keystone with a single carved urn in relief on a separate piece of marble – a motif repeated again and again throughout Robert Adam's designs (fig 146) and once more possibly signifying an association with the river gods.

fig 144

fig 145

(below)fig 146

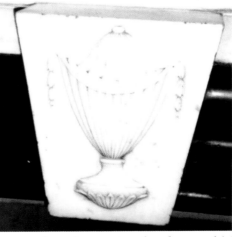

With a final glance upward at the spectacular dome which we shall not see again from the inside on our tour, we descend the six steps from the mezzanine floor and turn eastwards along the corridor (K) to the small staircase at the far (east) end ready to climb it to the second floor.

6
Second floor

Before we take the narrow staircase at the eastern end of the first floor corridor (K) a second glance out of one of the sash windows facing north reveals immediately below us the remains of the large archway which was the relocated entrance to part of the original yard and coach house from High Street (fig 48). The staircase in front of us (fig 145) has nine treads after which a turn to the left and a few more winders takes us to the second floor (fig 146).

fig 145

Immediately on the left, a door leads to the attic via another narrow staircase (fig 147). The attic was always a storage area for books, costumes and gymnasium equipment (fig 148). Once there, however, even in the dim light it is obvious that the area once had skylights but these were boarded over during refurbishments in the 1980s (fig 149). These skylights looked out onto the High Street but would have been hidden from view by the parapet which runs the total length of the building front and back. In the attic, plaster casts of various architectural mouldings were found when being cleared ready for sale in 2008. Some appear in the Appendix.

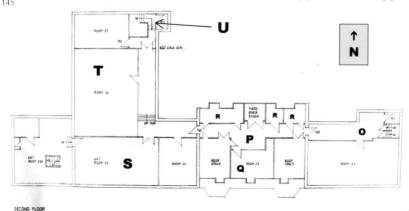

fig 146

fig 147   fig 148   fig 149

Descending the short flight of steps from the attic, we come again to the extreme east end of the second storey corridor (O). As we walk along it the windows on the northern side give us again a good view of the second rainwater head bearing the initials of the Rev John Halls and his wife, and the date 1755. This is in an exactly corresponding position to the one on the west wall seen earlier when the garden was being explored.

On the southern side of this corridor (O) a door opens into one large room (later made into two) with six small sash windows. The room is very plain with no important decorative features, but would have made a large workroom for the nuns and an excellent classroom for Colchester County High School.

As we continue westwards along this corridor, we come to the point where we step out of the 1904 east wing extension into the original 1755 house (P) and its servants' quarters. This point is marked by a sudden change in the direction of the floorboards. Those in the direction of travel along the corridor are parallel with our path, and those in the older part of the house are at right-angles to this. This apparent contradiction occurs also on the western side (fig 150). This photograph also shows two of the original early radiators on the left. There are only small windows in this corridor, which face the High Street, giving little light and no view because they open onto the rear of the parapet (fig 151).

An apparently insignificant feature, yet highly important, appears in this area. The servants' staircase, whose position we have traced from the ground floor upwards, emerges here outside the servants' bedrooms and storage rooms. The white-painted hand rail at the top of the servants' staircase has been carefully preserved because it was confirmed by English Heritage to be Chinese Chippendale, and could not be moved or altered in any way when a site for a lift was being considered by the college to enable the building to conform to requirements for the disabled (fig 152). The top exit of the stair well however, has been boarded over for safety reasons.

fig 150   fig 151   fig 152

Opposite the Chippendale handrail on the other side of this corridor the magnificent cast-iron furniture hoist can be seen folded back into its resting position against the glazed doors above the main stairwell, which we noted from the mezzanine floor below (fig 153). In operation it would have swung round through the open glazed double doors to lift furniture from the inner hall to the first or second floors.

The original Garraways sales catalogue of 1813 lists the building as having four servants' bedrooms. It seems likely that the four small doors on the north side of this corridor (two each side of the furniture hoist) would have been the four box-like servants' bedrooms (R). It was here that charred remains of the fire which occurred shortly after the Girls' High School took residence in 1920 were found in the form of a partially-burned ventilation duct. Each of the rooms has a small dormer window heavily surrounded by lead flashings on the outside and with no view because each one looks out onto the hipped roof of the Rev John Halls' 1780 extension. This will be seen more clearly from a window further along the west wing.

On the other hand, the north side of this area (P) has two doors (originally three) which lead into a narrow but long space (Q) which could originally have been three or four small rooms – it was quite usual for servants to share bedrooms or have dormitories of box-like proportions. There are only three small windows in this space, which look out towards the High Street, but are hidden by the parapet (fig 154). It is possible that this might have been the alternative servants' sleeping quarters instead of those on the opposite side of the corridor, but certain features are contradictory to this theory.

fig 153 LPP

fig 154

fig 155

Firstly, there is a small fireplace at the eastern end of this space - servants did not usually have the luxury of an open fire in their bedrooms (fig 155). The fireplace is immediately adjacent to the top of the servants' staircase (recently described), where fuel would have been brought up from the basement to stoke the fire. This heat was perhaps required for airing the bed-linen rather than for keeping the servants warm. It is therefore more likely that this area adjoining the south side of the upper corridor was a storage area for bed-linen and chamber pots and the other equipment necessary for servicing the bedrooms in the C18th. Another piece of evidence to support this theory is the opposing direction of the floorboards in the corridor outside, which suggests that there perhaps might have been some structural alterations here when the 1780 extension was added.

We continue westwards, leaving the 1755 section of the house and enter the 1904 wing at this second storey level. Another small window on the south side (similar to fig 151) looks out onto the parapet. It is inevitable that the top corridor with its dark, rather gloomy central section should have led to ghost stories through the generations. The 'Ghost of Grey Friars' was common knowledge to the girls of Colchester County High School as were stories of imaginative priest holes and secret tunnels. Such was the acceptance that there was a phantom, that compositions were often set in English lessons – sometimes in the manner of an illustrated medieval puzzle book, or even to make it more challenging, a written piece in French (see Appendix). One caretaker in the days of the Adult Community College insisted that his dog which always accompanied him on his last security rounds at night had, apparently, fled away howling from the top corridor having felt a threatening presence - the dog would never go with him again.

Ron Abbott (at Grey Friars 1959-61) transferring from St James' School to Grey Friars as temporary accommodation for Monkwick Secondary after CCHS moved out, writes – "On the upper floor there was a hinged ventilation door to a dark void built within the outside wall and it would sometimes blow open. We boys would tease the girls by telling them that there was a ghost in there … … there would be lots of screams from them, and this would make the boys laugh."

As we return to the top floor and the western corridor we see two doors on the High Street side, the first of which leads into a small room similar to the one added in the corresponding position in the east wing. The second door leads into a much larger room. Between them they share six small sash windows in total and have no decorative features.

Before entering this final large room we look to the right to see a flight of six steps leading up to a wider corridor at a different level (fig 156). This is to give the floor below added height and in turn to give the ground floor more height also, in order to house the high ceiling of the nuns' imposing chapel added in 1904 – this we will explore at the end of our tour.

We now enter the large room which was used as an art room in the days of the Adult Community College (S). It is light and airy and our instinct tells us that there must be an attic at this western end of the building to correspond with that at the eastern end – but there is no staircase. However, a hatch in the ceiling of this art room reveals a substantial un-floored attic space with supporting beams and a window looking towards Colchester Castle (fig 157).

fig 156   fig 157

This large art room, however, has a more interesting feature. A door at the western end reveals, when opened, a flight of five oak steps (fig 158) leading down to a lower room which is the second floor of the house next door – Hillcrest. The handrails on either side of this stairway reveal that the wall between the two houses is very thick – but in fact it is only partly a wall, the rest being a hollow void. This hollow space represents the original right-of-way between Grey Friars and Hillcrest. When the French nuns arrived in 1904 one of their first tasks was to join the two buildings together. This area was seen when we were in the garden, and more will be explained when we return once more to the ground floor.

Almost in the centre of this Hillcrest room, the top of its original staircase can be seen (fig 159), now with a balustrade for protection (fig 160). This may have been an additional staircase – as will be seen later – because this room also has a cast-iron solid fuel kitchen range finished in green enamel circa 1900 (fig 161) which suggests that this might have been a second floor kitchen at one time, or even separate accommodation in the form of a flat.

fig 158   fig 159

Colchester County High School used this room as an annexe to the main building, and domestic science was taught to accompany the more academic subjects and to prepare girls for life and marriage. But this was not until the late 1940s when the old-fashioned kitchen range would have been superseded by something more modern, although it still remained in place.

fig 160 LPP   fig 161

Ruth Lindsey (CCHS 1939-1949) writes –
"As it happened, for the first time ever, the Lower Sixth was offered a Home Science group for one year with Miss Easton. An old flat situated over the caretaker's house at Grey Friars (Hillcrest) had been converted for this purpose. A group of about eight of us became the Lower Sixth Home Science Group."

We retrace our steps and exit from Hillcrest and the large art room of Grey Friars until we are at the base of the short flight of steps which takes us to a slightly higher level at right angles to the corridor which we have just left.

If we look out of either of the two sash windows on our right in this short corridor there is a very good view of the hemispherical glass dome, and in the foreground, two of the lead-clad dormer windows of the former servants' quarters (fig 162). Once more, there is a view of a rainwater head with date and initials.

Still walking in a northerly direction we enter the door on our left and discover a very large room (T), with four sash windows on the west wall looking out again, towards Colchester Castle. The room is high with a vaulted ceiling whose span is supported by a tie-beam and a king post (fig 163).

fig 162   fig 163

> *Owen Hay remembers working on the dome: "In 1989 I was General Manager of the Glass Division at Kent Blaxill and Co., a position that gave me the opportunity to visit places and see areas of buildings not seen by the general public. It was always a pleasure to visit historic buildings such as Grey Friars, and appreciate what the craftsmen of the past could achieve without the benefit of modern equipment and see how the buildings survived the many changes of use they had experienced. Although the dome would have been glazed originally with curved glass to match the frame it was re-glazed with flat glass, no doubt a cost-cutting decision, but not an easy task." His colleague Ron Harvey worked on the dome; "Not the easiest of jobs, but he was glad to be back on site as he attended Grey Friars as a pupil whilst Monkwick School was being completed in 1958."*

This obviously would have made a very substantial work room for the nuns, a secluded classroom a long way from authority for the senior girls of Colchester County High School and a quiet, spacious and peaceful room for yoga classes of the Adult Community College. The space is matched by the room on the first floor immediately below (made into two rooms during the time of the adult college) and by the chapel on the ground floor which is even larger.

We leave this room and turn left along the corridor still walking northwards, passing the smaller adjoining classroom at the top of the wide back staircase (U) which is much more modern-looking than any of the previous stairways encountered in the rest of the building (fig 164). It is of course part of the 1904 extension. It is built in spiral fashion and at every five or six treads it takes a turn to the left with a small landing. This is repeated five times to reach the ground floor. At each floor and each main landing there is a small room matching the one at the top of the stairs, which has windows looking out to west and north (fig 165). On the eastward side at each bend small cupboards were converted into toilets at the time of the County High School.

fig 164   fig 165

If we descend the staircase to the first floor and glance along the corridor to the right (south) we can register that it is a mirror image of the short corridor above, which we have just left. We can see the short flight of descending steps at the end of this corridor matched by those on the floor above, giving height to the rooms below.

We continue to descend the wide back staircase with its dark oak handrail and plain unturned white-painted balusters, until we reach the ground floor and face the back door. Here we pause and gaze upwards at the impressive stair well which spirals upwards – many others of this period were painted at their apex to depict the heavens.

We take a turn to the left and after passing some storage cupboards under the stairs we come to another external door which leads out to a yard which was originally part of the garden.

7
Hillcrest and the Hall

Having passed through this minor entrance to the north we turn left along a concrete path. The area to our right is the remains of the original garden and the wall on our left which adjoins the path along which we are walking is the north wall of the nuns' chapel. This was part of the western extension constructed by the nuns. The County High School used it as a gymnasium and assembly hall and the Adult Community College used it for physical activities ranging from Scottish country dancing to flower arranging. Historical documents on the history of this corner of Colchester give conflicting evidence of the exact date that occupation of Grey Friars by the Sisters of Nazareth took place. We are told from an article written and researched by P. Manley aged 12 in the CCHS school magazine of 1946/47 that the nuns, whilst building proceeded, directed the builders through an iron grille. The only man allowed into the building was Dr Nicholson from Gate House, and only the lay sisters were allowed out. We also are told from research by the late Enid Bishop, Principal of the Adult Community College from 1973 to 1982, that whilst the building works were in progress the nuns are thought to have settled first at the Minories, before eventually moving to Grey Friars when they opened the school.

However, there can be no doubt that the chapel whose northern wall we are now passing had its stone laid (or perhaps was consecrated) in 1904 because a stone plaque set into the brickwork here on the outside is inscribed JMJ (Jesus, Mary Joseph) 1904 and has a Greek cross above (fig 166).

fig 166

fig 167

Looking up we now see two elaborate and colourful Edwardian stained glass windows with the letters JMJ repeated and incorporated into the pattern. More of these will be seen inside. A few more paces along the path is the back entrance to the adjoining small house, Hillcrest (fig 167). The rampant ivy here partly obscures the commemorative plaque and one of the stained glass windows. The first of the two doors leads into the northern end of the Hall where there is a slightly raised stage. This was obviously the altar end of the chapel. But we will take the second door which marks the position of the former right-of-way between Grey Friars and Hillcrest. And as we open the door and walk along the rather gloomy corridor we are following the former boundary between the buildings which were joined together by the nuns.

Fig 168 shows the area prior to 1904, and fig 168b shows it as it was in 2008.

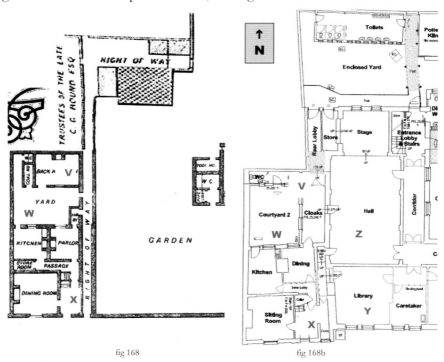

fig 168   fig 168b

The corridor we are now following runs alongside the western wall of the chapel and it is therefore no surprise when on the right we see a piscina (V) – a holy water basin in which the chalice was washed (fig 169). This was appropriately placed near the altar end of the chapel. It also suggests that perhaps the nuns lived mainly in the building of Hillcrest and used Grey

Friars as their workplace, school and religious centre – the chapel being the first room to pass through, participating in their morning service on their way into the main school.

fig 169

fig 170

We move out of this dark corridor once more into the open air and enter (W) a small completely enclosed back yard (fig 170) with the back door of Hillcrest in front of us. From here we can see more clearly the original position of the right-of-way and how it has been skilfully covered and incorporated into the two buildings (figs 171/2).

fig 171

fig 172

Two windows added into the brickwork on the ground floor give this corridor more light and the very slight differences in the shade of bricks indicate the junction between ground and first floors.

Having viewed this covered right-of-way from the outside it is time to retrace our steps and go inside again. Ignoring the passage to the north down which we came as we entered, we turn to the south and follow the right-of-way to the entrance hall of Hillcrest, immediately behind its front door (X). It is obvious that the window on the left beside the front door has been added to give additional light (fig 173). This is in the exact spot where the original right-of-way would have joined the High Street. The corresponding two 'windows' on the first and second floors are false (see fig 2).

fig 173   fig 174

In this hallway we notice the small but very fine quarter-turn staircase with winders (fig 174) which leads to the first floor landing. The plain wooden bannister with its white-painted balusters ends in an attractive spiral snail shape at its base (fig 175). Surprisingly, another door which appears to be a cupboard leads to a narrow dark staircase which emerges in the middle of the room adjoining the large art room on the top floor - as we have already seen.

Upstairs in Hillcrest the rooms are small, plain and insignificant, but in plan match those on the ground floor. Several alterations involving the joining together of rooms took place in order to convert the house into a crèche during the occupation of the Adult Community College.

One of the fireplaces on the first floor is, however, worth some attention. The cast iron grate is small and ornate and the surround plain (fig 176) but the vertical strips of tiles on either side are elaborate (figs 177 and 177b).

It appears to be a typical Victorian fireplace, perhaps added later after the building of Hillcrest in the late C18th. The use of tiles in an English domestic setting was rare in the C17th and C18th, but by the middle of the C19th they were becoming a major decorating feature. The variety of subject matter is far greater than that of any earlier or later period. Naturalistic flowers (as in the upper and lower tiles on each side of the fireplace) were common, as also were stylised flowers surrounded by a geometric border (as in the middle tiles on each side).

fig 175

fig 176

177 figs 177b

The first thought is that the installation of this fireplace might have coincided with the period when the Botanic Gardens were in operation (1824 to 1849), and interest in all things botanical was at its peak in Colchester, but the inclusion of the stylised sunflower within a border suggests the Aesthetic Movement of the 1870s and 1880s when the sunflower and peacock were dominant symbols of this era. Alternatively, they may be a very usual and common Victorian flower design.

However, they are of high quality, low relief and glazed, but it is very difficult to establish who manufactured or designed them. They are likely to be dust-pressed wall tiles, which are thinner and more porous than floor tiles. They may, or may not, be signed on the back, and we can only toy with a few names as influences or manufacturers.

During the middle 1800s, the firms of Pilkington, Minton and Morris, Marshall and Faulkner were producing tiles designed by Christopher Dresser (1834-1904), William de Morgan (1839-1917) and William Morris himself (1834-1896). Other manufacturers in this period included Copeland and Garrett, Maw and Co., Craven Dunnhill and Co. At this time, hand-crafted products were very desirable, mass production was frowned upon as was anonymity – but cheaper and inferior copies were also on the market. So the origin of these tiles in Hillcrest is very uncertain, but we can however, be certain that the designers of the day carried out extensive botanical studies of flowers and the underlying geometry of different specimens.

Many flower prints were also produced in this period because of the growing interest in gardens and the fashion for conservatories. It has already been established that the Rev John Halls' gardens at Grey Friars in the latter part of the C18th were magnificent and well-tended, and that there was an impressive conservatory. It is possible that those gardeners (famous or unknown) who followed in his footsteps during the C19th and early C20th might have been moved to commission a celebration in floral art on the tiles surrounding a fireplace. Did this happen here at Hillcrest? Ellen Willmott (1858-1934) a woman gardener and gatherer of foreign plants was a famous contemporary of Gertrude Jeykyll. Willmott lived not far away at Warley Place in Essex and was widely known – could she have been an influence?

Flowers in this period were often depicted as botanical jewels and valued for their rarity by plant collectors, and here on these four tiles at top and bottom either side of the fireplace the representation is so accurate that an expert could easily identify these specimens - woody stems, large white flowers with six petals, protruding stamens and leathery leaves rust brown on the underside. The details suggest that this is a variety of the evergreen magnolia (Magnolia Grandiflora) which was a well-known foreign import (fig 177c) having been brought to Britain from North America by the plant collector Mark Catersby in 1726. The number of petals (always a multiple of three) is often symbolic, and white represents the Virgin's purity – very appropriate as a decorative feature in part of a Franciscan nuns' residence at the beginning of the C20th. A similar spray of flowers appears in the O'Brien Thomas tile manufacturer's catalogue of 1891.

fig 177c

Having diverged into the world of botany we leave the small front entrance hall of Hillcrest by making an about-turn around a recent partition so that we are still within the covered right-of-way. A few steps northwards bring us to a door on the right and what appears to be the open framework at the rear of a cupboard. As we stand adjacent to the partition, we are level with the southern end of the large Hall of Grey Friars – previously the chapel. What appears to be the partially-dismantled back of a cupboard is, in fact, the nuns' confessional box – the door of which opens into the chapel – to be visited shortly.

Opening the door which we previously noticed adjoining the back of the confessional box, we mount two steps and find ourselves back in the main building of Grey Friars. The large room (Y) which we now enter was a workshop for the nuns, alongside which was a narrow mosaic-floored corridor forming an internal walkway from Hillcrest into Grey Friars for the nuns.

The combination of these two spaces made a science laboratory for Colchester County High School which had rows of hardwood benches, inset sinks and Bunsen burner taps. It later became a typing room for the Adult Community College and even later a library dedicated to the memory of Councillor Derek Lamberth, a good friend of the College and long-standing Chairman of Governors. A small part of this room was partitioned off at this time and together with a former fume cupboard became a caretaker's office.

At this point, double doors lead us into the junction of two corridors. Looking eastwards along the first one we can see in the distance the inner front entrance hall and the base of the main staircase which is where we started our tour. Looking straight ahead we see another identical corridor running alongside the eastern wall of the chapel. At the far end we see the small back entrance hall and the base of the spiral back staircase. This corridor has large sash windows on the right looking out to a courtyard. The wall on the left has six high-level windows with lead tracery which give additional borrowed light to the chapel (fig 178). The two corridors have the same mosaic floor with Grecian crosses and fret borders as we have already seen, and whichever way you look doorways are surmounted by semi-lunar windows to give even more light (fig 179).

fig 178

fig 179

We now enter the main hall (Z) through double doors at the rear which are on our left. We are immediately struck by its size and height (fig 180) achieved by elevating the rooms and corridors above on the first and second floors.

County High School, Colchester – Hall. (Greyfriars)

fig 180

As a chapel for the nuns this hall served its purpose admirably, and for an assembly hall for Colchester County High School it was more than adequate for the numbers on roll at that time.

It was adapted for a gymnasium by adding rib stalls at the southern end and on part of the west wall where a further panelled door led into an equipment cupboard. It was also ideal for Keep Fit and Dance classes when the building was occupied by the Adult Community College classes.

Joan Watson, Pat Grainge and Delia Bloom recall that CCHS often had visiting speakers and concerts by well-known musicians, and the assembly hall was where these took place.

Some time during 1943/44 Walter de la Mare came, and Pat says "I seem to remember sitting on the floor in the assembly hall listening to an elderly gentleman reading some of his poems to us. We had to be quiet and only clap at the very end." Joan adds of the visit, "I thought all famous poets were dead poets."

De la Mare (1873-1958) would have been about 70 at this time. 20 years earlier he had collected other people's poetry into a volume entitled Come Hither, widely used in schools, so he may have read some poems from this to the High School girls. In his own work he wrote about the English sea, coast and nature, as well as some supernatural subjects, which would have had an appeal for children at the time.

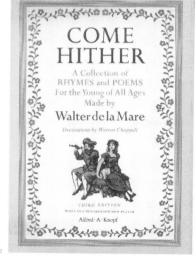

Walter de la Mare

Several ex-pupils of CCHS have been inspired to write. One of these was Pamela Brown, CCHS 1936-39, author of The Swish of the Curtain (see Appendix).

185

The high level windows on the eastern side which we saw from the adjoining corridor are matched by high level windows on the west side of the hall. These again are decorated with lead tracery forming the shapes of flowers in bud. All of these high level windows have a complex metal winding system (still in place) for opening them (fig 181). The floor has the original hardwood parquet blocks – now over 100 years old (fig 182).

fig 181

fig 182

fig 183

In the south-eastern corner of the hall it is now possible to see the small panelled door to the nuns' confessional box (fig 183), the back of which was visible as we re-entered Grey Friars from Hillcrest. If this door is opened it emerges that the original glass panel with its tracery matching that of the high-level windows has been boarded over and is now hidden from view (fig 184).

fig 184

fig 185

Looking up, the chapel ceiling is far from plain. Raised ribs divide the area into sections – squares, rectangles and octagons to form a coffered ceiling (fig 185). It is pleasing to think that possibly when the nuns designed this they were always intending to decorate each panel with a mural as many famous chapel ceilings were enhanced.

Beyond a wide archway, and elevated on a low platform, the north end is the highlight of this former chapel. This would have been the altar end which is close to the door into Hillcrest where the piscina is situated.

The two Edwardian stained glass windows (which, like the plainer ones, owe much to the art nouveau designs of the period - fig 186) earlier seen from the outside can now be seen in all their glory with the light shining through them.

Red, blue, yellow and brown stained glass is divided by lead tracery and the curvaceous pattern is repeated extensively. Between the two windows there is a tall arched alcove with a lower panelled three-sided projecting plinth shaped like an oriel window which would originally have held a religious figure (fig 186).

186 LPP

Centrally in each window JMJ appears enclosed by a stylised flower shape (fig 187).

fig 187

189

And so we reach the end of our tour. But it is appropriate that we finish here in the hub of the building. How many thousands of feet have passed this way along the three mosaic-floored corridors which bear the signs of the nuns' occupation in the Greek crosses scattered within the design underfoot! One corridor (covered at the time of writing by carpet) leads eastwards from Hillcrest, one leads westwards from the imposing front door, and one leads southwards from the back door and the garden. All converge on the former chapel at the heart of the present building.

Here the nuns would have celebrated their last religious service in 1920 before the building was handed over to Essex County Council who allocated it to Colchester County High School. The girls and staff of CCHS assembled here in 1957 for the last time as they sang the school hymn "God Be in My Head" before moving on to their new building in Norman Way.

And finally the students, tutors and support staff of the Adult Community College gathered in here in 2007 to pay tribute to the history of the building over a Heritage Open Weekend when guided tours gave many people the opportunity to say goodbye to a much-loved establishment.

Now in 2014, after a careful and sensitive restoration it is about to enter another life, its eighth; but like many other old buildings, its fascination lies not only in what it reveals to us, but also in what it conceals from us.

Here within these pages, we, the authors, have presented you with what we have discovered. We hope that you will join us in the ongoing project by visiting www.greyfriarscolchester.org.uk where more information and memories can be found, and you can contribute.

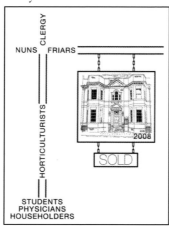

Glossary

ACANTHUS — A plant with thick-lobed leaves, the image of which is used in architectural, carved and moulded ornaments.

ADAM, Robert 1728-1792 — British architect, decorator and furniture designer of the late 18th century.

ADJOINED PILLAR — A pillar or column which is not entirely free-standing, but has a small portion attached to a wall.

AESTHETIC MOVEMENT — A movement in art/architecture of the 1870s/80s which believed in the supremacy of the beautiful, using the peacock and sunflower as its most popular motifs.

ANTIQUARY — Student and/or collector of antiques, antiquaries and allied information.

APSE — A semi-circular or polygonal extension to a larger rectangular area, often with a rounded vault above.

ARCHITRAVE — The lintel extending from one column to another, and the lowest of the three main parts of an entablature.

ARMATURE — A metal or wooden internal support or framework for a sculpture modelled in soft clay, wax or plaster-of-Paris.

ART NOUVEAU — A style of decorative art in vogue circa 1880 to 1914, characterised by curved and expressive lines, flower and leaf motifs.

BALUSTRADE — A series of short posts or pillars supporting a rail.

BANNISTER — A staircase rail, as above.

BAY WINDOW — A window in a curved or angled projection from a house wall and, if curved, often called a bow window.

BRACE — Subsidiary timbers set diagonally to strengthen the wooden frame which supports a roof.

BUTTRESS — Stonework, brick or other masonry built against an existing wall and projecting from it in order to counteract the outward thrust.

CANOPY — A hood of any material projecting from a wall as a covering or shelter.

CAPITAL — The uppermost and wider part of a pillar, column or pilaster which supports the entablature above.

CASTELLATED — An architectural term used to describe a building decorated with battlements.

CHIPPENDALE, Thomas 1718-1779 — English furniture maker and designer noted for his neo-classical, neo-gothic and chinoiserie styles.

CLASSICISM — A return to the rules of artistic law and order and the principles of Greek and Roman architecture.

COBBETT, William 1763-1835 — Son of a farmer, home-educated journalist, radical, MP, best known for 'Rural Rides' (1830) which is still in print today.

COFFERED CEILING — Ceiling decoration consisting of sunken squares or polygonal ornamental panels.

COLLAR BEAM — A horizontal transverse beam connecting a pair of rafters at a height below the apex of a roof.

COLUMN — A round, square or rectangular upright structure, normally acting as a support and composed of one solid piece or a series of drums.

COMPOSITE — The most elaborate of the classical orders whose capital combines the scrolls and acanthus leaves of the two lower orders, together with other decorative motifs.

CORBEL — A projecting block or bracket which supports a horizontal beam.

CORINTHIAN — One of the classical orders identified by the acanthus leaf decoration on its capital.

CORNICE — The uppermost section of a classical entablature.

COVING — A wide, decorative moulding concealing the junction between the walls and ceiling of a room.

DADO RAIL — A wooden rail at chair-back height around the walls of a room to prevent potential damage caused by the movement of chairs.

DAME SCHOOL — Small private school for young children run by women often in their own home; precursors of nursery/infant schools; existed in England possibly before the C16th century in both towns and rural areas and survived into the C19th century.

DENTILS — Series of small ornamental tooth-like blocks used in classical decorative mouldings.

DOME — A vault of even curvature over a circular or square base.

DORIC — One of the simplest and earliest of classical orders which is sparsely decorated.

DRESSER, Christopher 1834-1904 — English designer and writer on the decorative arts, particularly in household objects such as wallpapers, furniture, metalwork, pottery, glass and textiles.

DRUM	A circular vertical wall supporting a dome.
EGG AND DART	A decorative moulding based on a pattern of alternate eggs and arrow-heads.
ENTABLATURE	In classical architecture, the upper part of an order consisting of the architrave, frieze and cornice.
FANLIGHT	A window over a door, mainly in Georgian buildings.
FLUTING	Shallow, concave, decorative grooves running vertically on the shafts of columns and other surfaces.
FRET	A geometric ornament or moulding composed of horizontal and vertical lines repeated to form a border or band.
FRIEZE	The middle section of an entablature between the architrave and the cornice.
GEORGIAN ARCHITECTURE	Historical division of English architecture, 1714-1880 in the reigns of Georges I, II, III and IV.
GESSO	A paste composition of gypsum, glue and water which hardens into a solid, and is used for mouldings on walls, ceilings, furniture and picture frames.
GIBBONS, Grinling 1648-1721	English Baroque sculptor known for his decorative carvings of flowers, leaves and fruit in wood, marble and stone.
GOTHIC	The style of architecture in Europe which came between the Romanesque and Renaissance and characterised by pointed arches, rib vaults and flying buttresses.
GREEK CROSS	A cross with four equal-length arms at right-angles to one another.
GREENAWAY, Kate 1846-1901	Illustrator of children's books for which she often supplied the text.
HIPPED ROOF	A roof which has sloped instead of vertical ends.
IONIC	One of the classical orders, characterised by the spiral volutes in its capital.
JONES, Inigo 1573-1652	British architect who imported the classical style from Italy together with Palladian details.
JEKYLL, Gertrude 1843-1932	Artist, craftswoman, photographer, writer and influential garden designer.
KENT, William 1685-1748	English painter, furniture designer, landscape gardener and architect.
KEYSTONE	The central stone at the crown of an arch or rib vault, which is often carved.
KINGPOST	A vertical beam standing centrally on a tie or collar-beam, and meeting the apex of a roof where it supports the ridge.
MEDALLION	A circular or oval decorative motif, often part of the mouldings on a doorway or window.
METOPE	The square section between the triglyphs in the frieze of the Doric order.
MEZZANINE	A middle storey inserted between two higher ones.
MODILLIONS	A series of small scrolls or brackets beneath a cornice.
MORGAN, William de 1839-1917	English pottery designer particularly noted for his decorative plates and tiles.
MORRIS, William 1834-1896	English poet and political theorist, designer and craftsman in the late Victorian decorative arts.
MOSAIC	A picture or pattern made from small pieces of coloured glass or stone set into cement or plaster.
MOULDING	A decorative strip used on walls, furniture and picture frames, either carved from wood or made from plaster, gesso or stucco.
MULLION	The vertical post dividing a window into two or more lights.
NEO-CLASSICISM	The radical phase of late 18th century classicism.
NEO GOTHIC	The movement in the very late C18th/19th to revive the Gothic style of architecture.
NEWEL	The principal post and its balusters at the end of a flight of stairs.
OFSTED	Office for Standards in Education – the government's inspectors.
ORDERS	In classical architecture, the orders consist of variations on a standard plan made up of a column, a capital and an entablature. The five orders are: Tuscan, Doric, Ionic, Corinthian and Composite.
ORIEL WINDOW	An upper-storey overhanging window supported on corbels.
OVERMANTEL	Ornamental structure in wood or plasterwork over a mantelpiece.
PALLADIANISM	Style of architecture derived from buildings and publications of Andrea Palladio.
PALLADIO, Andrea 1508-1580	Influential Italian architect who aimed to recapture the splendour of antiquity and to revive Roman symmetrical planning.

PALMETTE	A type of classical decorative motif which is fan-shaped, and may resemble a palm leaf or honeysuckle flower.
PARAPET	A low wall, sometimes castellated, intended as a protection against a sudden drop.
PARTERRE	Formal garden on level surface, consisting of planting beds, typically in symmetrical patterns, separated and connected by edged gravel paths
PATERA	Small circular flower-like discs.
PAXTON, Joseph 1803-1865	English architect and landscape architect who worked in glass and metal roof construction and who designed the Crystal Palace.
PEDIMENT	A triangular or low-pitched gable above a door, window or portico.
PEVSNER, Nicolaus 1902-1983	German-born British scholar of history of art/architecture best known for his 46-volume The Buildings of England (1951–74), often simply referred to as "Pevsner".
PIANO NOBILE	The principal floor above the ground floor in grand town or country houses, which contains the reception rooms.
PILASTER	An ornamental pillar or column represented as a flat form attached to a wall and projecting from it without a supporting function.
PISCINA	A stone basin with a drain, free-standing or against a wall, and near the altar, for washing the Communion or Mass vessels.
RELIEF	A sculpture or moulding made so that all or part of it projects from a flat surface.
RIB	Projecting band on ceiling or vault which can be functional, structural or purely decorative.
RISER	The vertical surface of a step.
RUNNING DOG	A classical ornament or moulding, similar to the image of a breaking wave, and sometimes called the Vitruvian scroll.
SASH WINDOW	A window, double-hung with wooden sashes which allow it to slide up and down in vertical grooves by means of pulleys.
SEMI-LUNAR WINDOW	A half-moon shaped window.
SERLIANA	A window named after its designer and often called a Venetian window.
SERLIO, Sebastiano 1475-1554	Italian painter and architect, and the author of the first practical and theoretical book on architecture, "L'architettura", published posthumously 1584.
SHAFT	The central section of a column or pilaster between the capital and the base.
SOANE, Sir John 1753-1837	English architect with a very personal neo-classical style which combined unexpected spatial interplay with complexity and severity.
STAINED GLASS	Translucent coloured glass set between a framework of lead tracery to form a decorative or pictorial design and used in windows.
STRINGING COURSE	Projecting horizontal band of brick or stone running across exterior of a building.
STUCCO	A plaster made of lime and pulverised marble which is carved and chiselled for sculpture and architectural decoration. It is often confused with gesso, which is made of gypsum, not lime, and is much softer.
SWAG	A decorative festoon, often of flowers or leaves, which imitates the form of a piece of material draped over two supports.
TESSELLATED FLOOR	A mosaic of small cubes of marble, pottery, brick, glass, tile or stone set in mortar.
TIE-BEAM	The main horizontal beam which carries the ends of the principal rafters at wall level in a roof.
TRACERY	The ornamental intersecting work, often in lead, used in a window.
TRANSEPT	The transverse arms of a cross-shaped church between the nave and the chancel.
TREAD	The horizontal surface of a step.
TRIGLYPH	Small, decorative blocks separating the metopes in a Doric frieze.
TUSCAN	Style of architecture which is the simplest form in the hierarchy of classical orders.
URN	An oval, covered vase used for retaining the ashes of the dead, but often used as a decorative motif in architectural interiors.
VAULT	An arched ceiling over a space in a building.
VENETIAN WINDOW	In classical architecture, a window of three lights, the central one arched and flanked by two lower rectangular ones.
VITRUVIUS POLLIO, Marcus (active 46-30BC)	Ancient Roman architect/theorist whose treatise on architecture, 'De Architectura' had an enormous influence on design from the early Renaissance onwards.
VOLUTE	A spiral scroll-shape found in an Ionic capital.
WINDER	A staircase tread, wider at one end than the other.
WIRE, William 1804-1857	Self-educated skilled artisan, antiquary, diarist 1842-1857 (see Appendix)

Acknowledgements

Many thanks are due to the following galleries, organisations, businesses and individuals who have generously given permission for drawings, plans, images and diagrams to be reproduced.

Alison Woolnough (AW), Bridget Nelson (BN), Colchester Archaeological Trust (CAT), Colchester and Ipswich Museum Services (CIMS), Colchester County High School for Girls (CCHS), The Courtauld Gallery (CG), Dick Joice Bygones Museum Holkham Hall (DJM), English Heritage – Kenwood House (KH), Essex County Newspapers (ECN), Essex County Record Office (ECRO), Howard Leyshon (HL), Julie Graham (JG), Lawson Planning Partnership (LPP), Linda Michael (LM), OMC Investments Ltd (OMCI), Purcell, Miller, Tritton (PMT), Reeman Dansie Auctions (RD), Vestry House Museum (VHM).

Many of the early postcards are from the Joan Gurney collection. Some images or parts of images come from photographs taken for the Adult Community College by Stephanie Mackrill Photography and Harland Payne Photo. All other colour and monochrome photographs come from contributions through the Sharing Heritage project, from the former Grandad's Photography Museum, East Hill, Colchester, or from the collections of (or taken by) Joan Gurney and Alan Skinner, except where noted.

A few illustrations, some of unknown source, many of which have been provided by contributors from home and abroad during this wide-reaching community education project, are believed to be free of copyright, but the authors, c/o the CALA Charity, would be pleased to hear from any unacknowledged source, photographer, individual or organisation.

The authors wish to acknowledge the work of the late Rev Mrs Jill Newham, whose initial and detailed research 25 years ago enthused and guided them in this project.

Very many others have helped in numerous ways and offered support, guidance and encouragement, giving freely of their time and knowledge. These include Dr John Ashdown-Hill, Philip Crummy and Don Shimmin of the Colchester Archaeological Trust, Peter Froste, Dr Michael Leach, Jess Jephcott, Robert Marks, Richard Humphreys of Humphrey's Weaving Co Sudbury, Marion Williams, Yvonne Carter, Terry Bird, Juliet and Tony Crick, Bob Everitt, Mike Shute, Diana Hargrave, Yvonne Watts, Julie Wilde, Sheila Scott, Valerie Denniss, Simon Gallup, Beth Chatto, Jo Edwards, Matthew Tanton Brown, CCHS Old Girls'/Alumnae Association. Thanks are also due to Sylvia Skinner and Gerald Gurney not only for their patience and tolerance over seven years of book preparation, but also for proofreading duties.

Finally, the authors wish to record their appreciation of the time given by all those who have supplied memories and information. Further contributions are acknowledged and/or featured on the accompanying website www.greyfriarscolchester.org where updating of this research takes place. Everyone with an interest in Grey Friars is encouraged to visit the website and take part in the ongoing project. We are sure there is much more to discover regarding this fascinating part of our historic town.

Sources of information
and
guide to further reading and research

Ashdown-Hill, John *Mediaeval Colchester's Lost Landmarks* Breedon Books 2009

Beltramini, Guido & Burns, H (eds) *Palladio* Royal Academy of Arts 2008
Bensusan-Butt, J *The House that Boggis built, A social history of the Minories, Colchester* Victor Batte-Lay Trust 1989
Britnell, Richard *Colchester in the Early Fifteenth Century – a portrait*
http://www.dur.ac.uk/r.h.britnell/Colchester/Portrait_of_Colchester.htm
Brown, AFJ *Essex People 1750–1900 from their diaries, memoirs & letters* Essex Record Off Publ no 59 1972
Brown, AM *Colchester County High School, The first 50 years* 1961

Christou, Panaghiotis & Papastamatis, K *Greek Mythology* Bonechi 2008
Clarke, Michael *The Concise Oxford Dictionary of Art Terms* 2001
Colchester Archaeological Trust (CAT) *journal: The Colchester Archaeologist, Report 391: An archaeological desk-based assessment of land around the Adult Community College, Grey Friars, High St, Colchester, Essex* November 2006 *and website* www.cat.essex.ac.uk
Colchester County High School *Magazine* 1946-1947
Cromwell, Thomas *History and Antiquities of the Ancient Town and Borough of Colchester* London, 1825
Crummy, Philip *City of Victory – the story of Colchester – Britain's first Roman town* CAT 1997
Crummy, Philip *The lost friary of Grey Friars* The Colchester Archaeologist number 20, CAT 2007

Davidson Cragoe, Carol *How to read buildings, a crash course in architecture* Herbert Press 2008
D'Cruze, S *A Pleasing Prospect - Social change and urban culture in C18th Colchester* U of Herts Press, 2008
Denney, Patrick *The Buildings of Colchester through time* Amberley Publishing 2012
Dept of Environment *List of buildings of special architectural or historical interest, Borough of Colchester volume 1*

Earl of Leicester *Holkham* 2004
English Heritage *Kenwood, The Iveagh Bequest* 2010/14; *Chiswick House & Gdns* 2007; *Kenwood Restored* 2014

Fleming J, Honour H, & Pevsner N *The Penguin Dictionary of Architecture and Landscape Architecture* 1999
Fleming, John & Honour, H *The Penguin Dictionary of Decorative Arts* 1979

Garwood, Ivan *Mistley in the Days of the Rigbys* Lucas Books 2003
Goose, Nigel & Cooper, Janet *Tudor and Stuart Colchester* Victoria County History of Essex 1998
Guardian and Observer *Guides to British Architecture part 1 476AD-1700 & part 2 1720-present* Sept 2001
Gurney, Joan *Pictures from the Past – Memories of Colchester County High School* Access Books 2009

Hall, James *Hall's Dictionary of Subjects and Symbols in Art* John Murray 1996
Hedges, J & Denney, P *Starvation or Surrender – Matthew Carter's Siege of Colchester* 2002
Herbert, Tony & Huggins, K *The Decorative Tile* Phaedon 1995
Historical Royal Palaces *The Banqueting House* 2000
History of the County of Essex: Vol 9: The Borough of Colchester www.british-history.ac.uk
Hope Moncrieff, AR *Classic Myth and Legend* Gresham Publishing Company
Howarth, Eva *Crash Course in Architecture* Caxton Editions 2001
Hughes, Therle *The pocket book of furniture* County Life 1968
Hull, MR *Roman Colchester* Society of Antiquaries 1958

Jones, Joan *Minton. The first two hundred years of design and production* Swan Hill Press 1993
Jones, Owen *The Grammar of Ornament* Herbert Press London 2008

van Lemmen, Hans *Victorian Tiles* Shire Publications Ltd 1995

Lloyd, Nathaniel *History of the English House* Architectural Press London 1975
Lockett, Terence *Collecting Victorian Tiles* Antique Collectors' Club 1979

Mander, D *Images of Essex, The Photographs of Alfred Wire* Vestry House/Alan Sutton Publishing 1995
Martin, Geoffrey *The Story of Colchester from Roman Times to the Present Day* Benham 1959
Mollett JW *Dictionary of Art and Archaeology* Bracken Books 1994
Mowl, Timothy *William Kent, Architect, Designer, Opportunist* Pimlico 2007

Orr, Kate *An archaeological evaluation in the car park of Grey Friars Community College* CAT 2003

Pearson, Catherine (ed) *EJ Rudsdale's Journals of Wartime Colchester* The History Press 2010

Rice, Matthew *Rice's Architectural Primer* Bloomsbury 2009
Richardson, OP *Guide to Colchester – A short history and guide* 1961
Round, JH *Lionel de Bradenham and Colchester* Paper of 1913 CAT Report no 39 cat.essex.ac.uk

Schwarz D, Freeman M, Skinner A *Grey Friars – Opening the Door to Adult Education* Access Books 2005
Stoughton Hyde, Lilian *Favourite Greek Myths* D C Heath and Co 1923
Summerson, John *The Classical Language of Architecture* Thames and Hudson 2012

Tames, Richard *Robert Adam* Shire Publications Ltd 2008
Trustees of Sir John Soane's Museum *A New Description of Sir John Soane's Museum* 2007

University of London Institute of Historical Research *The Victoria County History of Essex* OUP

Wilde, Julie *The Botanic Gardens in Colchester – a degree research paper* 2001
Worsley, Lucy *If Walls could Talk* Faber and Faber 2011

Tracing the history, land use, occupants and development of the Grey Friars site in Colchester is an on-going community learning project by the educational charity CALA (Colchester Adult Learning Assistance). The website

www.greyfriarscolchester.org

provides further information, research findings, material to share and an opportunity to participate.

Appendix

Page 95   Silk worms will eat the leaves of both the white and black mulberry trees together with oak and lettuce leaves, but only the white mulberry leaves allow them to produce silk of the correct textile strength because of the high sericen content in them; one acre of ground planted with white mulberries, three feet apart, will only produce one kilo of silk from the silkworms fed on leaves. In addition, the climate of this country is not suitable for the production of good quality silk. The King of France, Louis XIII, however, persuaded James I to plant black mulberries all over Great Britain (there are several round about the Grey Friars site) in the belief that a silk trade could be developed here. This false information was a strategy used to avoid the threat to the silk trade of France. It is very unlikely, therefore, that the nuns who occupied Grey Friars from 1904 to 1920, and who were good embroiderers, had "home-grown" silk. It undoubtedly was imported from China, and the pupils of CCHS who reared silk worms on black mulberry leaves produced such low-grade silk that the whole breeding process for them was just an exercise in natural history.

Page 107   This house interior is an early- to mid- C18th watercolour "The Drawing Room" 17" x 24" (fig 28b). It is possibly Earlham Hall, a Gurney family house, now part of the University of East Anglia. The artist is unknown.

Page 115   Some interesting discoveries in the cellars when the building was cleared in 2008 included pulleys, hooks and gas mantels (above). Nothing was found of an equestrian nature despite the cellars being partly below the original coach house, yard and stables.

Page 118   Desks at CCHS (fig 52) in the 1920s and 1930s were very old-fashioned. They were made of a dark-stained wood, and had an atlas rack at the front and an inset ceramic ink well in the right-hand corner which adjoined a long shallow groove to take pencils. The ink wells were regularly replenished with ink from a can with a long spout – but they became very battered and chipped (below).

Page 119 The Mathematics Mistress is a pencil drawing by Jean Alexander (fig 52b). Jean Dryden Alexander was born in 1911 at Priest's Cottage, Shenfield, Essex. She studied at Chelmsford Art School between 1928 and 1931, going on afterwards to the Slade School from 1931-1935. She then returned to Essex in 1936 to take up a teaching post at Brentwood County High School, becoming head of the art department until her retirement in 1970. From 1970 to 1974 she lived in New Zealand where she continued to teach art, returning to East Anglia in 1974 to live at Thelveton near Diss, and start an art group there. She exhibited at the Royal Academy, the New English Art Club and the Society of Women Artists.

Page 124 Andromeda is an oil sketch on board by Sir Alfred James Munnings 1878 – 1959 (fig 58b). This is a study of a standing female nude 61cm x 46.5cm. It was purchased in the late 1960s by a gentleman, from another Dedham man nicknamed "Tosser", who had posed for Munnings in the 1960s as a jockey and had been given the painting by Sir Alfred who lived in Dedham. When Tosser married, his wife had objected to the painting hanging in their home, and he therefore sold it. It was re-sold by Colchester's Reeman Dansie auctions, in November 2013.

Page 168 A selection of plaster mouldings were found in the attic. These are much larger than any which appear on doors, walls, ceilings and windows, so it is unlikely that they date from the C18th. Many of them have a small metal loop for hanging / display and some of them have a number impressed, or other means of identification. The larger ones have an armature with hessian padding. A selection of other mouldings were found with these.

An egg-and-dart moulding marked 2739   A dentil moulding impressed with DENTIC VI

Page 129 Some of the pieces of furniture in the Headmistress's study of CCHS (fig 66) formerly the library of the Rev John Halls' house, are now in the CCHS archive at Norman Way. Below: roll-top desk, armchair, rail-back chair and small occasional table from the study, and an umbrella stand which stood near an entrance.

Page 135 The illustration shows a pair of battledores, the heads of which are composed of a hollow 'drum' of vellum – an alternative to strings. The lower image shows an ink inscription added to the 'throat' of the battledore which records that Pippa and Mary kept up a rally of 1500 strokes on 15th February 1889.

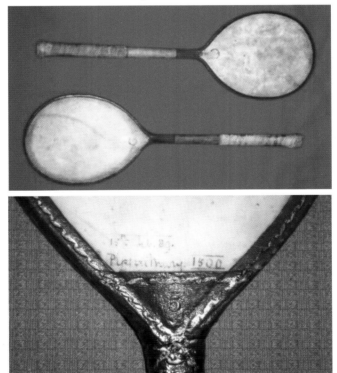

Page 140   This small pocket rosary made of silver and coral was found under the floorboards in Grey Friars by the carpenter renovating joists. It might have belonged to one of the nuns (or novice nuns) during the time that it was a priory (1904-1920), or even to one of the young girls who were boarders when the nuns opened a school there. JMJ appears on the central medallion.

< 9cm >

Page 154   Robert Adam's use of sky-blue paint on panelled doors at Kenwood House in 1760 (below) was reflected throughout Grey Friars when redecorated in the 1980s (fig 109 et al)

KH

200

March 9th

Histoire de Revenants

Jeanne demeurait à la campagne dans une grande ferme qui était hantée. Une nuit orageuse quand Jeanne était au lit elle entendit un bruit. Elle sauta en bas du lit et elle mit sa robe mais elle n'alluma pas. Elle écouta! Il n'y eut pas de son. Alors elle entendit un fracas et alors un gémissement. Elle frémit! Qu'était-ce? Alors une fumée blanche et transparente vint par un trou de la serrure et prit forme. C'était un revenant. La fantôme grimaça. Il plaça une main mince visqueuse sur l'épaule de Jeanne. Elle frémit! Le fantôme dit, d'une voix aiguë, "Je suis le spectre du chauffeur qui fut assassiné. Je hante cette maison. Au revoir". Le fantôme disparut et Jeanne entendit un autre gémissement. Alors elle sauta dans le lit et tira l'édredon sur la tête.

Ghost Story.   Jeanne lived in the country in a big farmhouse which was haunted. One stormy night when Jeanne was in bed she heard a noise. She jumped out of bed and put on her dressing gown, but didn't turn on the light. She listened. There wasn't a sound. Then she heard a crash and the sound of someone moaning. She trembled! What was it? Then a white, transparent mist came in through the key hole and took shape. It was a ghost. The spectre grimaced. It put a thin, sticky hand on Jeanne's shoulder. She trembled! The ghost said in a high-pitched voice, "I am the ghost of the driver who was murdered. I haunt this house. Good bye." The ghost disappeared and Jeanne heard another moan. So she jumped into bed and pulled the eiderdown over her head.

Page 185   Pamela Brown CCHS 1936-1939. This famous author of many books for children was born in Colchester in December 1924. She attended Colchester County High School until 1939 when, at the outbreak of the Second World War, she was evacuated to her extended family in Wales. She had started writing "The Swish of the Curtain" in 1938, when she was just thirteen years old. She sent successive chapters of the book to the friends she had left behind in Colchester, but the book was not published by Nelson until 1941, after the manuscript was saved from the publisher's offices when they were bombed in the blitz. She trained as an actress at RADA adopting the stage name Mela Brown. Later she produced many programmes for children's television. Her last TV appearance was on Blue Peter in the early 1980s when she met young actors and actresses who were appearing in the television adaptation of her first book. These children included Sarah Greene who later became a presenter of Blue Peter. Pamela Brown married David Masters, also an actor, in 1949. She died in Hampshire in January 1989. The Swish of the Curtain is still in print.

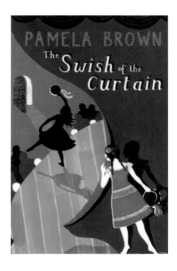

Of "The Swish of the Curtain", Dame Eileen Atkins has said: "An enchanting book. A must for any child who wants to become an actor." Dame Maggie Smith said, "I wanted to act before I read this book, and afterwards there was no stopping me." Longwater Books now reproduces these books in their original form, without abridgements or modern amendments.

End papers   The end papers of this book were taken from a picture by Cecily Griffiths who used the well-loved ancient Holm Oak in the gardens of Grey Friars as her centrepiece. Cecily was in one of the Adult Community College's art classes at the time, with Howard Leyshon as the tutor.

Additional finds when the floorboards were lifted: We are grateful to the carpenter who passed these items on to us – a fascinating collection of social detritus across the decades …

Full list of items. Coins: sixpences of 1959, 1963, 1967; pennies of 1919 x2; halfpenny (ha'pny) of 1966. There was also a used, franked, torn George V scarlet penny stamp (1918-21?).

School-related items: pen knib, Wm Toplis, Sheffield from ink dip pen; ruler, named Edna Cox Upper IV; an ESA plastic desk ink well sliding lid; maths test paper named Marie Leighton Lower 4B; Geography test paper named David Trelau 1B; History tests named Alec Shave 2B and Iain Stephen 2a; scrap of paper with the name Madeline Vallis 3B; defaced poem, 'Six and Out' by G.D. Martineau; two 'burials' of creatures unknown in folded and sealed paper pockets.

Scraps of paper and card items: Paper bag from Broom's of North Hill; Guarantee tag for electrical installation W.T.Henley's Telegraph Works Co Ltd, North Woolwich London E; Burton credit scheme leaflet giving examples of credit terms in £/s/d; Kangol beret wash label; Essex County Council receipt for £49 (decimal currency); Visiting card "The Coltown Syndicate" Manager DJL Cant, 32 Winston Avenue, Shrub End; "Amendment Record Card" 1948 A.P.4280.D with entries for A.L. numbers 21-23 21 on July 64, A.L. number 24 on 12.11.64, and A.L. number 25 on 12.11.??.

Smoking-related items: empty packet for 20 Wills Gold Flake cigarettes; empty cigarette papers packet, "Papier A G from Paris, all printing in French; Cigarette cards – Churchmans 'Westminster Hall' from the King's Coronation Series; Players – Robert 'Beau' fielding from the 'Dandies' series; Lew Ayres from the Film Stars series.

Post cards, both un-sent: Grey Friars Convent (photographic, very early 1900s scene, soon after building the extensions?) addressed to Mesdamoiselles Rickling, Pensionnan Nazareth, Enghien, Hainaut, Belgique. Some writing around the edge of the photograph, but no message on the reverse; plus a much-defaced and torn view of Lexden Road in tramway days.

William Wire (1804-1857) This man is worthy of special note in this book, because in his relentless pursual of knowledge, always in the context of recording and sharing, and despite lacking a privileged education in younger life, he exemplifies the 'Grey Friars' ethos from its period as an adult college.

William Wire
"The Postman's Tale" by Andrew Phillips, full text in the Colchester Archaeologist no 11 1998 ©

Andrew Phillips wrote "William Wire qualifies as Colchester's first archaeologist. While previous antiquarians like Stukely or Morant wrote history largely based on written sources, it was 100 years later that the extraordinary Wire systematically investigated and recorded Colchester's buried archaeological remains – and quite a lot were being uncovered and destroyed in his day. Wire was from an old Colchester family: weavers, freemen of the borough and sturdy Radicals in politics ... born in Colchester ... apprenticed in London as a watchmaker ... with poor health struggled to raise a large family on the profits of a retail workshop ... withdrew from active politics as Chartism became more militant. He attended lectures in the town and himself presented a paper to the Society of Antiquaries in London. Wire's learning was outstanding, but local antiquarians were disposed against him because of his social class.

However, 'his shop (in Church Street) was a place of resort for many leading men of science and technology' and 'for the next 25 years there passed through his hands the chief bulk of the coins, urns, and Roman remains found in the town ...' Above all, from 1842 until his death in 1857, Wire kept a detailed record in diary form of all his archaeological findings in the town , and these constitute essential sources for all subsequent archaeology. Wire died aged only 52, his last years dogged by disappointment and illness. Late in life William Wire was recognised as one of the more remarkable figures in the town despite his humble station. *Note* - **Alfred P. Wire 1839 - 1914** All Wire's thoroughness in recording these findings would be nothing if one of his sons, Alfred P. Wire, a schoolmaster and himself an active antiquarian, had not donated all his father's papers to Colchester." Alfred Wire's photographs form the content of the book "Images of Essex" by David Mander. One of his photos features the section of High Street including Grey Friars in 1903.

About the authors

Photograph: Essex County Newspapers

Neither Joan Gurney nor Alan Skinner are academic historians, but they do have a passionate interest in local history and adult education. They are therefore delighted that their research on Grey Friars has fired local people's imagination and has become an on-going community education project in its own right. Lectures on various themes are available and everyone can participate through the website: www.greyfriarscolchester.org

Joan has enjoyed a very long association with Grey Friars. She has lived in the Colchester area all her life, except for the years of study at university. She entered the Preparatory Department of CCHS in 1938, progressed through the Junior and Senior Departments, leaving in 1951. After training as a teacher, she taught in various local secondary schools, attending several evening classes at Grey Friars when it became the Adult Education Centre.

In 1971 she transferred to adult education and became a Senior Tutor at the re-designated Adult Community College where she remained until 2003. She believes that her unusual combination of subject qualifications – biology, physical education, sociology, swimming teaching and, more recently, history of art – has given her a unique insight into the story of Grey Friars. She is also a compulsive collector, not only of early postcards, but of bathing bygones, of which her archive and expertise have national significance.

Alan came to Colchester in 1983 to be the Principal at Grey Friars. Originally from London, with degrees from the University of Birmingham, the Open University and a teaching qualification from the University of London, he has had a varied career, most of it spent in education, 36 years of which were with Essex County Council.

In the late 1980s he moved into adult education full time from his position as Head of the English Department in a comprehensive school. Having taught evening classes since his first teaching post in the 1960s he was well aware of the value of learning throughout life and became a strong campaigner for adult education, locally and nationally. As well as being at Grey Friars for 22 years, he has been a governor of local schools, chaired the Colchester Learning Shop partnership and assisted educational charities. In the year 2000 Birthday Honours, H.M. Queen Elizabeth II presented him with the MBE for services to education.

Access Books is the publishing arm of **CALA** charity number 1095713
Colchester **A**dult **L**earning **A**ssistance • encouraging and supporting local adult education

Still available:

Grey Friars –
Opening the Door to Adult Education
by D. Schwarz, M. Freeman, A. Skinner
Foreword by Baroness Helena Kennedy QC
The story of the adult college told through
inspirational examples from just a few of the
tens of thousands of people who have gone
through the blue door to learn, work or
support the education of adults in Colchester.

•

Pictures from the Past –
Memories of Colchester County High School
by Joan Gurney - A lavishly-illustrated book
based on postcards produced in the 1920s
supported by fascinating anecdotes from when
Grey Friars and North Hill were the two centres
of Colchester County High School for Girls.

•

Ginny Saunderson • E.Joan Gray
The story of a family living in London in the
first half of the C20th. Joan, a long-standing
student at Grey Friars in its days as an adult
college, tells of a 'good' childhood in a period
of adversity, poverty, war - before the NHS.
Authenticity of period detail and vivid recall
make this a riveting read.

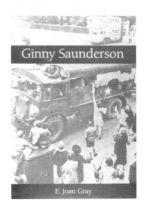

•

For further details of these and other publications
from this adult education charity, visit the website
www.greyfriarscolchester.org.uk
or email
access.books@btinternet.com

Do you have any further knowledge of Grey Friars?

If so, please share it on **www.greyfriarscolchester.org.uk**

Giant Holme Oak (Evergreen)
at Grey Friars, Colchester.